HAMLYN'S ALL-COLOUR BOOK OF

Quick Dishes

HAMLYN

LONDON · NEW YORK · SYDNEY · TORONTO

Acknowledgements
Recipes created by Moya Maynard
Photography by John Lee
Cover picture by Iain Reid
Artwork by John Scott Martin
China kindly loaned by Josiah Wedgwood and Sons Limited,
Royal Doulton Tableware Limited and Denby Tableware
Limited

Published by
The Hamlyn Publishing Group Limited
London · New York · Sydney · Toronto
Astronaut House, Feltham, Middlesex, England

ISBN 0 600 37417 3

Printed in Spain by Printer industria gráfica sa
Sant Vicenç dels Horts   Barcelona   1978
Depósito Legal B. 745-1978

Contents

Introduction

For a quick meal many people automatically think of omelettes and snacks on toast which are nutritious, quick and easy to prepare, but with a little imagination and this book as your guide you will see that the range of dishes is far greater.

In order to produce quick meals at a moment's notice make sure that you have certain basics in your store cupboard – pasta, canned meats and fish, tomato purée, canned fruit, soups (canned and packaged) which can be used when making a speedy casserole, canned vegetables, a selection of seasonings and herbs, stock cubes and mayonnaise. There are many ways for freezer owners to overcome the worry of quick meals. For example, certain basics can be made and frozen in advance and these can be utilised when required. Partly-baked flan cases, basic sauces such as bolognaise for serving with pasta, cooked pancakes frozen in layers with dividers ready to be filled and reheated. Of course many dishes may be completed in advance and frozen, only requiring to be reheated. Even sandwiches may be frozen, a great boon particularly if you have to provide packed lunches. Hard-boiled eggs and salad vegetables are about the only sandwich fillings which do not freeze successfully, but there are many others which can be used – grated cheese and chutney, liver sausage, cream cheese with flavourings, canned sardines, salmon or tuna or cold sliced meats, to name a few.

Even when time is short try not to forget the appearance of the final dish. The simplest of garnishes makes all the difference and it takes only seconds to make a garnish of parsley by snipping a few sprigs of parsley with a pair of scissors over the dish – much quicker than chopping the parsley on a board. By looking at the way the dishes are presented in the book you will see how your garnishes can be varied.

With this book as your guide, coupled with your own imagination, you will soon find your repertoire of quick meals and snack ideas much wider than before.

Useful facts and figures

Notes on metrication

In this book quantities are given in metric, imperial and American measures. Exact conversion from imperial to metric measures does not usually give very convenient working quantities and so the metric measures have been rounded off into units of 25 grams. The table below shows the recommended equivalents.

Ounces	Approx. g to nearest whole figure	Recommended conversion to nearest unit of 25
1	28	25
2	57	50
3	85	75
4	113	100
5	142	150
6	170	175
7	198	200
8	227	225
9	255	250
10	283	275
11	312	300
12	340	350
13	368	375
14	397	400
15	425	425
16 (1 lb)	454	450
17	482	475
18	510	500
19	539	550
20	567	575

Note: When converting quantities over 20 oz first add the appropriate figures in the centre column, then adjust to the nearest unit of 25. As a general guide, 1 kg (1000 g) equals 2.2 lb or about 2 lb 3 oz. This method of conversion gives good results in nearly all cases but in certain pastry recipes a more accurate conversion is necessary to produce a balanced recipe. On the other hand, quantities of such ingredients as vegetables, fruit, meat and fish which are not critical are rounded off to the nearest quarter of a kg as this is how they are likely to be purchased.

Liquid measures The millilitre has been used in this book and the following table gives a few examples:

Imperial	Approx. ml to nearest whole figure	Recommended ml
¼ pint	142	150 ml
½ pint	283	300 ml
¾ pint	425	450 ml
1 pint	567	600 ml
1½ pints	851	900 ml
1¾ pints	992	1000 ml (1 litre)

Note: For quantities of 1¾ pints and over we have used litres and fractions of a litre.

Spoon measures All spoon measures given in this book are level.

Can sizes At present, cans are marked with the exact (usually to the nearest whole number) metric equivalent of the imperial weight of the contents, so we have followed this practice when giving can sizes.

Oven temperatures
The table below gives recommended equivalents.

	°F	°C	Gas Mark
Very cool	225	110	¼
	250	120	½
Cool	275	140	1
	300	150	2
Moderate	325	160	3
	350	180	4
Moderately hot	375	190	5
	400	200	6
Hot	425	220	7
	450	230	8
Very hot	475	240	9

Note: When making any of the recipes in this book, only follow one set of measures as they are not interchangeable.

Notes for American users
Although the recipes in this book give American measures, the lists below give some equivalents or substitutes for terms and commodities which may be unfamiliar to American readers.

Equipment and terms
BRITISH / AMERICAN

frying pan / skillet
greaseproof paper / wax paper
grill / broil
kitchen paper / paper towels
liquidise / blend
mince / grind
packet / package
stoned / pitted

Ingredients
BRITISH / AMERICAN

aubergine / eggplant
beetroot / beet
chipolatas / link sausages
chipped potatoes / French fries
cornflour / cornstarch
courgettes / zucchini
demerara sugar / brown sugar
double cream / heavy cream
gammon steaks / smoked ham slices
hard-boiled eggs / hardcooked eggs
marrow / summer squash
minced beef / ground beef
pepper / sweet pepper
plain flour / all-purpose flour
plain chocolate / semi-sweet chocolate
spring onion / scallion
streaky bacon rashers / bacon slices
sultanas / seedless white raisins
sweetcorn / corn kernels
Swiss roll / jelly roll
tomato ketchup / tomato catsup
tomato purée / tomato paste
unsalted butter / sweet butter
vanilla essence / vanilla extract
veal escalopes / veal scallops

Notes for Australian users
Ingredients in this book are given in cup, metric and imperial measures. In Australia the American 8-oz measuring cup is used in conjunction with the imperial pint of 20 fluid ounces. It is most important to remember that the Australian tablespoon differs from both the British and American tablespoons; the table below gives a comparison between the standard tablespoons used in the three countries. The British standard tablespoon holds 17·7 millilitres, the American 14·2 millilitres, and the Australian 20 millilitres. A teaspoon holds approximately 5 millilitres in all three countries.

British	American	Australian
1 teaspoon	1 teaspoon	1 teaspoon
1 tablespoon	1 tablespoon	1 tablespoon
2 tablespoons	3 tablespoons	2 tablespoons
3½ tablespoons	4 tablespoons	3 tablespoons
4 tablespoons	5 tablespoons	3½ tablespoons

Soups and starters

This section gives a selection of exciting first course recipes which should be suitable to serve for a family meal or when entertaining. None of the recipes are lengthy to prepare or cook, yet they will impress your family and guests. By looking at the pictures alongside the recipes you will be able to see how to garnish and present these dishes.

Tomato and corn soup with garlic toast

METRIC/IMPERIAL/AMERICAN
75 g/3 oz/¾ cup onion, chopped
2 teaspoons corn oil
1 (298-g/10½-oz/10½-oz) can condensed tomato soup
300 ml/½ pint/1¼ cups milk
1 tablespoon tomato purée
1 (198-g/7-oz/7-oz) can sweetcorn with peppers
GARLIC TOAST
50 g/2 oz/¼ cup butter
1 large clove garlic, crushed
salt and pepper
4 slices medium sliced bread

Place the onion and oil in a pan and cook very slowly for 5 minutes until soft without browning. Stir in the soup, milk and tomato purée and mix until the ingredients are thoroughly blended. Add the sweetcorn with the liquor and cook gently, uncovered, for 10–15 minutes.

Meanwhile, make the garlic toast by blending the butter, garlic and seasoning together. Spread half the mixture on one side of each piece of bread, and toast under the grill. Spread the remaining butter mixture on the uncooked side and toast. Remove the crusts and cut in half before serving with the soup.

Serves 4

Blue cheese and cauliflower soup

METRIC/IMPERIAL/AMERICAN
1 medium cauliflower
225 g/8 oz/2 cups onion, chopped
1 litre/1¾ pints/4¼ cups chicken stock
pepper
40 g/1½ oz/3 tablespoons unsalted butter
25 g/1 oz/¼ cup plain flour
50 g/2 oz/½ cup Danish blue cheese, crumbled
GARNISH:
chopped parsley
fried croûtons

Prepare the cauliflower and break into sprigs. Place in a large pan with the onion, stock and pepper. Cover and cook slowly for 10–15 minutes until the vegetables are tender. Cool slightly, then sieve or liquidise until smooth.

Melt the butter in a saucepan, stir in the flour and cook gently for a few seconds. Gradually stir in the cauliflower purée, bring to the boil and cook for about 3 minutes.

Add the cheese, a little at a time, until completely dissolved. Garnish each bowl of soup with chopped parsley and serve with fried croûtons.

Serves 6

Sweetcorn and cucumber salad

METRIC/IMPERIAL/AMERICAN
½ cucumber, peeled
1 teaspoon salt
1 (198-g/7-oz/7-oz) can sweetcorn
2 teaspoons grated onion
150 ml/¼ pint/⅔ cup soured cream
pepper
mint sprigs to garnish

Coarsely grate the cucumber, put on a plate and sprinkle with salt; leave to stand for at least 30 minutes. Drain off excess water from the cucumber using kitchen paper.

Mix the drained corn and the cucumber together in a bowl with the grated onion. Pour off any excess liquid from the soured cream, then stir into the cucumber mixture with some freshly ground pepper.

Place in serving dishes and garnish with the mint.

Serves 4

Egg mayonnaise

METRIC/IMPERIAL/AMERICAN
½ box mustard and cress
4 hard-boiled eggs
6 tablespoons/6 tablespoons/½ cup mayonnaise
2 tablespoons/2 tablespoons/3 tablespoons single cream
GARNISH:
4 anchovy fillets
mustard and cress

Trim the mustard and cress and wash carefully in a colander. Drain well then arrange on individual plates. Shell the eggs and cut in half lengthways. Place the cut side down on the mustard and cress.

Mix the mayonnaise and single cream together, spoon over the eggs to cover. Drain the anchovy fillets well on kitchen paper and cut in half lengthways. Garnish with the anchovy fillets and mustard and cress.

Serves 4

Carrot and celery salad

METRIC/IMPERIAL/AMERICAN
150 ml/¼ pint/⅔ cup soured cream
1 teaspoon lemon juice
¼ teaspoon salt
¼ teaspoon pepper
2 tablespoons/2 tablespoons/3 tablespoons mayonnaise
225 g/8 oz/1⅓ cups celery or celeriac, chopped
100 g/4 oz/⅔ cup carrots, peeled and grated
1 tablespoon chopped parsley to garnish

Place the soured cream, lemon juice, salt, pepper and mayonnaise in a mixing bowl and blend thoroughly. Place the celery and carrot in a serving dish and pour the soured cream dressing down the centre. Sprinkle with the parsley and serve immediately.
Note: This starter could also be served as a side salad to a main meal.

Serves 4

Sardine and beetroot salad

METRIC/IMPERIAL/AMERICAN
1 small lettuce
225 g/8 oz/1½ cups cooked beetroot, peeled and diced
1 (125-g/4¼-oz/4¼-oz) can sardines in oil
salt and pepper
pinch mustard powder
pinch castor sugar
2 tablespoons/2 tablespoons/3 tablespoons oil
1 tablespoon vinegar
1 small onion

Wash the lettuce leaves, drain well and shred very finely. Arrange on 4 individual plates. Divide the beetroot between the plates.

Drain the oil from the sardines, carefully remove the bone from each and divide between the dishes, arranging the sardines with the skin side uppermost.

Place the seasonings and sugar in a small bowl, stir in the oil and gradually beat in the vinegar a little at a time. Pour a little of this dressing over each salad. Slice the onion finely into rings and place a few on top of each salad.

Serves 4

Tuna salad

METRIC/IMPERIAL/AMERICAN
1 (198-g/7-oz/7-oz) can tuna
50 g/2 oz/½ cup onion, finely sliced
150 ml/¼ pint/⅔ cup soured cream
2 tablespoons/2 tablespoons/3 tablespoons mayonnaise
salt and pepper
GARNISH:
slices of cucumber
slices of tomato
anchovy fillets
stuffed olives

Drain the tuna well, place in a bowl and break up the flesh with a fork. Add the onion with the soured cream, mayonnaise and seasoning to taste.

Arrange cucumber and tomato slices alternately around the edge of a dish, then pile the fish mixture in the centre. Garnish with well-drained anchovy fillets, arranged in a lattice over the top, and sliced olives.

Serves 6

Florida cocktail

METRIC/IMPERIAL/AMERICAN
2 large oranges
1 grapefruit
4 tomatoes
salt and pepper
pinch mustard powder
pinch castor sugar
4 tablespoons/4 tablespoons/⅓ cup oil
2 tablespoons/2 tablespoons/3 tablespoons white wine
    vinegar
mint sprigs to garnish

Using a sharp knife, remove the rind and pith from the oranges and grapefruit and cut out the segments from in between the membrane. Place in a bowl with the skinned, quartered and deseeded tomatoes.

Place the seasonings in a bowl, stir in the oil and gradually add the vinegar, mixing well. Pour the dressing over the fruit mixture. Serve in individual dishes, garnished with a sprig of mint.

Serves 4

Grilled ginger grapefruit

METRIC/IMPERIAL/AMERICAN
2 grapefruit
2 tablespoons/2 tablespoons/3 tablespoons ginger wine
50 g/2 oz/¼ cup demerara sugar
25 g/1 oz/1 oz stem or preserved ginger, chopped
mint sprigs to garnish

Cut the grapefruit in half and, using a serrated grapefruit knife, cut between the membrane of each segment. Cut round the grapefruit to release the segments from the pith. Carefully lift out the membrane leaving the segments in place. Sprinkle each half with a little of the ginger wine, sugar and chopped ginger.

Preheat a moderate grill. Remove the rack from the grill pan and place the fruit cut side uppermost in the pan. Cook until the sugar melts without burning the grapefruit. Garnish with the mint and serve.

Serves 4

Spicy prawn cocktail

METRIC/IMPERIAL/AMERICAN

1 small lettuce
6 tablespoons/6 tablespoons/½ cup mayonnaise
2 tablespoons/2 tablespoons/3 tablespoons tomato
   ketchup
1 teaspoon Worcestershire sauce
dash Tabasco sauce
2 teaspoons creamed horseradish sauce
225 g/8 oz/1⅓ cups peeled prawns

Wash and dry the lettuce leaves. Line 4 serving dishes with the
leaves.

Mix the mayonnaise, tomato ketchup, Worcestershire sauce,
Tabasco and horseradish sauce together until blended. Stir in
the prawns and divide mixture between the dishes.

Serves 4

Chicken liver and egg pâté

METRIC/IMPERIAL/AMERICAN

50 g/2 oz/¼ cup butter or margarine
2 medium onions, finely chopped
1 clove garlic, crushed
225 g/8 oz/½ lb chicken livers, trimmed
4 hard-boiled eggs
2 tablespoons/2 tablespoons/3 tablespoons sherry or
   brandy
salt and pepper
GARNISH:
slices of cucumber
mustard and cress

Melt the butter or margarine in a large frying pan. Add the
onion and garlic and cook very gently for about 10 minutes
until soft. Add the chicken livers and cook for about
10 minutes, stirring occasionally. Place in a mixing bowl.

Reserve one egg yolk for the garnish and put the remaining
shelled hard-boiled eggs through a mincer. Place in the bowl,
add the sherry or brandy and seasoning, and mix. Transfer to
individual dishes. Cover and chill in the refrigerator for several
hours before serving. Garnish with sliced cucumber, a
sprinkling of the reserved chopped egg yolk and mustard and
cress.

Serves 6–8

Fish dishes

When time is at a premium, fish makes an ideal choice for a meal as it does not require lengthy cooking. Use fresh fish on the same day it is purchased; if you do not have a reliable wet fishmonger in your area it is better to choose frozen fish which is processed within hours of being caught. For a speedy meal, make use of canned fish such as tuna and salmon which lend themselves to many tasty dishes.

Halibut with savoury butter

METRIC/IMPERIAL/AMERICAN
salt and pepper
3 halibut steaks
50 g/2 oz/¼ cup butter
2 tablespoons/2 tablespoons/3 tablespoons chopped fresh herbs (parsley, chives, thyme or summer savory)
1 tablespoon lemon juice
slices of lemon to garnish

Preheat a moderate grill. Lightly season the fish and place the butter on top. Put the fish in the grill pan (rack removed) and grill gently, turning once, for about 15 minutes depending on thickness. Remove the fish to a heated serving dish.

Pour the grill pan juices into a saucepan and add the herbs and lemon juice. Heat through, stirring, and spoon over the cooked fish. Serve immediately with French fried potatoes and garnished with lemon slices.

Serves 3

Crispy curried plaice

METRIC/IMPERIAL/AMERICAN
2 large plaice, filleted
salt and pepper
75 g/3 oz/$\frac{3}{4}$ cup flour
egg and breadcrumbs to coat
175–225 g/6–8 oz/1 cup long-grain rice
25 g/1 oz/2 tablespoons butter or margarine
1 clove garlic, crushed
50 g/2 oz/$\frac{1}{2}$ cup onion, chopped
2 teaspoons curry powder
$\frac{1}{2}$ teaspoon turmeric
600 ml/1 pint/2$\frac{1}{2}$ cups stock
$\frac{1}{2}$ teaspoon finely grated lemon rind
1 teaspoon marmalade
parsley sprig to garnish

Cut the plaice diagonally into strips. Season 25 g/1 oz/$\frac{1}{4}$ cup flour and use to coat the fish. Dip the fish in beaten egg, then toss in fresh or golden breadcrumbs.

Cook the rice in a pan of boiling salted water. Melt the butter or margarine, add the garlic and onion and cook until soft. Add the curry powder and turmeric. Stir in the remaining flour and blend in stock. Bring to the boil, stirring, simmer for 10 minutes. Stir in lemon rind, marmalade and seasoning.

Meanwhile, heat oil for deep frying and fry the plaice until crisp and golden; drain. Arrange the rice on a serving dish. Pile the fish on top and garnish. Serve the sauce separately with accompaniments illustrated.

Serves 4–6

Haddie omelette

METRIC/IMPERIAL/AMERICAN
225 g/8 oz/$\frac{1}{2}$ lb smoked haddock
25 g/1 oz/2 tablespoons butter
25 g/1 oz/$\frac{1}{4}$ cup flour
150 ml/$\frac{1}{4}$ pint/$\frac{2}{3}$ cup milk
1 (92-g/3$\frac{1}{4}$-oz/3$\frac{1}{4}$-oz) can peeled prawns, drained (optional)
1 tablespoon chopped parsley
1 teaspoon lemon juice
4 eggs
3 tablespoons/3 tablespoons/$\frac{1}{4}$ cup water
salt and pepper

Cover the fish with water and poach gently for 10 minutes. Drain, reserving 150 ml/$\frac{1}{4}$ pint/$\frac{2}{3}$ cup of the fish liquor. Remove the skin and bones from the fish and flake the flesh.

Melt the butter in a pan. Add the flour, stirring, and cook for 1 minute. Stir in the milk and reserved fish liquor, cook for 2 minutes. Stir in the flaked fish, prawns, parsley and lemon juice.

Separate yolks from whites of the eggs and place in separate bowls. Add the water and seasoning to yolks, beat thoroughly. Whisk the whites stiffly and fold into the yolk mixture.

Heat a little oil in an omelette pan and pour in half the egg mixture. Cook gently until the mixture sets. Place the pan under the grill and cook until the surface is golden. Turn out on to a hot plate, spoon half the sauce filling on top. Cook a second omelette, fill and serve.

Serves 2

Anchovy fish pie

METRIC/IMPERIAL/AMERICAN
4 frozen cod steaks, thawed
1 (64-g/2¼-oz/2¼-oz) packet instant potato
40 g/1½ oz/3 tablespoons butter
40 g/1½ oz/6 tablespoons plain flour
150 ml/¼ pint/⅔ cup milk
4 teaspoons anchovy essence
salt and pepper
2 large eggs, hard-boiled
50 g/2 oz/½ cup cheese, grated
melted butter
7 anchovy fillets
parsley sprigs to garnish

Cover the cod steaks with water and poach for 10–15 minutes. Drain, reserving 150 ml/¼ pint/⅔ cup of the fish stock.

Make up instant potato according to packet directions.

Melt the butter in a pan. Stir in the flour, cook for 1 minute and gradually add the reserved stock and milk. Bring to the boil, stirring, and simmer for 2 minutes. Stir in the anchovy essence, flaked fish and seasoning.

Pipe the potato around the edge of a large ovenproof dish. Halve the eggs and place in the bottom of the dish. Cover these with the fish sauce, sprinkle with the grated cheese. Brush the potato with melted butter. Cut the anchovy fillets in half lengthways and arrange in a lattice over the fish. Place under the grill and heat through for about 15 minutes. Garnish.

Serves 4

Trout with almonds

METRIC/IMPERIAL/AMERICAN
4 medium trout, gutted
4 tablespoons/4 tablespoons/¼ cup flour
salt and pepper
75 g/3 oz/6 tablespoons butter
2 tablespoons/2 tablespoons/3 tablespoons corn oil
75 g/3 oz/¾ cup blanched slivered almonds
1 tablespoon lemon juice
1 tablespoon chopped parsley
GARNISH:
twists of lemon
parsley sprigs

Wash the trout and wipe on kitchen paper. Remove the eyeballs and any fins. Put the flour on a plate and season with the salt and pepper. Coat the fish well in the seasoned flour and fry gently in 50 g/2 oz/¼ cup of the butter and the oil for about 5 minutes each side, depending on thickness of the fish. Remove the fish from the pan and keep hot.

Add the remaining butter to the pan, stir in the almonds and fry until lightly browned. Add the lemon juice and parsley, heat through for a few seconds.

Spoon the almond mixture over the trout. Serve immediately garnished with lemon twists and parsley sprigs.

Serves 4

Stuffed herrings with mustard sauce

METRIC/IMPERIAL/AMERICAN
1 (99-g/3½-oz/3½-oz) packet country stuffing mix
15 g/½ oz/1 tablespoon butter, melted
1 small apple, diced
4 medium herrings, cleaned and boned
SAUCE:
15 g/½ oz/1 tablespoon butter or margarine
1 small onion, chopped
1 teaspoon mustard powder
15 g/½ oz/2 tablespoons plain flour
300 ml/½ pint/1¼ cups milk
salt and pepper
watercress and lemon butterflies to garnish

Make up the stuffing according to the directions on the packet
and stir in the butter and apple. Divide the mixture between the
4 fish, spreading the filling along the length of each. Fold the
herrings over and place them in a buttered ovenproof dish.
Cover with foil and bake in the centre of a moderately hot oven
(190°C, 375°F, Gas Mark 5) for about 25–30 minutes.

Place butter or margarine in a saucepan, add the onion and
sauté gently without browning for about 5 minutes. Stir in the
mustard powder and cook gently for a further 5 minutes. Add
the flour and gradually stir in the milk. Bring to the boil and
simmer for 2 minutes. Season to taste and spoon over the fish or
serve separately. Garnish with watercress and lemon butterflies.

Serves 4

Tuna and macaroni bake

METRIC/IMPERIAL/AMERICAN
175 g/6 oz/1½ cups macaroni or pasta shells
2 eggs, hard-boiled
1 (198-g/7-oz/8-oz) can tuna
3 tomatoes
CHEESE SAUCE:
40 g/1½ oz/3 tablespoons butter or margarine
40 g/1½ oz/6 tablespoons plain flour
600 ml/1 pint/2½ cups milk
75 g/3 oz/¾ cup cheese, grated
salt and pepper
GARNISH:
slices of tomato
parsley sprig

Cook the pasta in plenty of boiling salted water for about 12
minutes until tender. Drain well. Shell and chop the eggs. Drain
the tuna. Slice the tomatoes.

Melt the butter or margarine in a saucepan, add the flour and
gradually beat in the milk. Bring to the boil stirring and cook
for 3 minutes. Stir in 50 g/2 oz/½ cup of the cheese and the pasta.
Taste and adjust the seasoning.

Arrange all the ingredients in layers in a deep casserole dish
finishing with a layer of sauce. Sprinkle the remaining cheese
over the top. Bake in the centre of a moderate oven (180°C,
350°F, Gas Mark 4) for 30 minutes. Garnish with sliced tomato
and parsley.

Serves 4–6

Tuna kedgeree

METRIC/IMPERIAL/AMERICAN
225 g/8 oz/generous cup long-grain rice
1 (198-g/7-oz/8-oz) can tuna
4 eggs, hard-boiled
75 g/3 oz/6 tablespoons butter or margarine
1 medium onion, chopped
7.5-cm/3-inch/3-inch length cucumber, peeled and diced
2 teaspoons lemon juice
1 tablespoon chopped parsley
salt and pepper
quartered cucumber slices to garnish

Cook the rice in a large saucepan of boiling salted water for 10–15 minutes until tender. Drain well.

Drain the liquid from the tuna and flake the fish. Remove the yolks from 2 of the eggs and sieve on to a plate. Chop the remaining eggs and whites.

Place the butter or margarine in a frying pan, add the onion and sauté for about 5 minutes until soft without browning. Stir in the cucumber and lemon juice and cook for a further 2 minutes. Stir in the rice, tuna, chopped egg and parsley. Season to taste. Heat through for about 5 minutes. Place in a heated serving dish, garnish with the sieved egg yolk sprinkled in the middle and quartered cucumber slices.

Serves 4

Scalloped kippers

METRIC/IMPERIAL/AMERICAN
2 medium kippers
50 g/2 oz/$\frac{1}{4}$ cup butter or margarine
25 g/1 oz/$\frac{1}{4}$ cup flour
300 ml/$\frac{1}{2}$ pint/1$\frac{1}{4}$ cups milk
salt and pepper
1 teaspoon lemon juice
4 stuffed olives, sliced
2 eggs, hard-boiled
1 tablespoon chopped parsley (optional)
1 (148-g/5$\frac{1}{4}$-oz/5$\frac{1}{4}$-oz) packet instant potato
twists of lemon and parsley sprigs to garnish

Cover kippers with water and poach for 10 minutes.

Make a sauce by melting 25 g/1 oz/2 tablespoons of the butter or margarine in a pan. Stir in the flour, cook for 1 minute and gradually add the milk. Bring to the boil and cook for 2 minutes, stirring.

Remove the flesh from the bones of the kippers; flake, and add to the sauce. Add seasoning to taste, lemon juice, sliced olives, coarsely chopped eggs and parsley, if used.

Divide the mixture between 4 scallop shells or individual flameproof dishes. Make up the instant potato according to the packet directions using the remaining 25 g/1 oz/2 tablespoons butter or margarine. Place in a piping bag and pipe potato around the edge of each dish. Place under a hot grill to heat through and brown. Garnish.

Serves 4

Creamed scallops

8 scallops, washed and quartered
150 ml/¼ pint/⅔ cup water
40 g/1½ oz/3 tablespoons butter
40 g/1½ oz/6 tablespoons plain flour
150 ml/¼ pint/⅔ cup milk
50 g/2 oz/½ cup button mushrooms, sliced
1 teaspoon chopped fresh fennel
1 teaspoon lemon juice
salt and pepper
1 (64-g/2¼-oz/2¼-oz) packet instant potato
parsley sprigs to garnish

Poach the scallops in the water for about 5 minutes until they become opaque. Remove with a slotted spoon and reserve the liquor.

To make the sauce, melt the butter in a saucepan, stir in the flour and cook for a few minutes. Gradually add the milk and reserved fish stock. Bring to the boil, stirring, and cook for 2 minutes. Stir in the mushrooms, fennel, lemon juice, scallops and seasoning.

Divide the mixture between 4 ovenproof dishes or scallop shells. Preheat a moderate grill.

Make up the instant potato according to the directions on the packet and pipe a border round the edge of each dish. Place under the grill to lightly brown the potato. Serve immediately garnished with the parsley.

Serves 4

Prawns creole

100 g/4 oz/generous ½ cup long-grain rice
1 medium onion, chopped
1 clove garlic, crushed
1 tablespoon oil
1 (227-g/8-oz/8-oz) can peeled tomatoes
½ small green pepper, deseeded and chopped
8 pimento-stuffed olives, halved
salt and pepper
350 g/12 oz/2 cups peeled prawns

Cook the rice in boiling salted water for about 10–15 minutes until just tender. Drain and keep hot.

Place the onion, garlic and oil in a saucepan, cook gently to soften without browning, about 5 minutes. Add the tomatoes, pepper, olives and seasoning to taste. Simmer for about 10 minutes to reduce the liquor. Stir in the prawns and heat through for 5 minutes.

Arrange the rice round the edge of a heated serving dish, pour the prawns creole in the centre.

Serves 3

Meat, offal and poultry dishes

There are many ways to prepare quick main meals. Choose cuts of meat which cook quickly and need little preparation such as frying steak, chops, cutlets and veal escalopes; also make use of canned meats such as corned beef. Minced beef is marvellous for quick meals as it can be transformed into a host of exciting meals.

Paprika beef

METRIC/IMPERIAL/AMERICAN
1 large onion, sliced
2 tablespoons/2 tablespoons/3 tablespoons oil
0.75 kg/1½ lb/1½ lb frying steak
1 green pepper
150 ml/¼ pint/⅔ cup beef stock
½–1 teaspoon paprika
pinch sugar
salt and pepper
2 canned red peppers
2 tablespoons/2 tablespoons/3 tablespoons plain flour

Place the onion in a large frying pan with the oil. Saute gently, without browning, for 5 minutes. Cut the frying steak into 4 pieces and fry quickly until lightly browned.

Remove the meat from the pan and arrange in an ovenproof casserole with the onion rings placed over the top. Slice the pepper, add to the pan and fry for 3 minutes. Remove and add to the casserole.

Stir the stock into the pan, add paprika, sugar and seasoning. Blend and add to the meat.

Drain and slice the canned red peppers and arrange over the meat. Cover the dish and cook in the centre of a moderate oven (180°C, 350°F, Gas Mark 4) for ½–1 hour until the meat is tender. When cooked, remove to a heated serving dish.

Pour the liquid into a small saucepan, blend the flour with a little water, add to the pan and bring to the boil, stirring. Cook for 3 minutes then pour over the meat. Serve with broccoli.

Serves 4

Betty's quick country steaks

METRIC/IMPERIAL/AMERICAN
40 g/1½ oz/3 tablespoons butter
1 medium onion, chopped
2 cloves garlic, crushed
100 g/4 oz/1 cup mushrooms, sliced
2 quick-frying steaks
2 teaspoons French mustard
salt and pepper
1 teaspoon Worcestershire sauce
1 teaspoon tomato purée
2 tablespoons/2 tablespoons/3 tablespoons chopped
    parsley

Melt the butter in a frying pan. Add the onion and garlic and cook slowly to brown and soften the onion. Add the mushrooms and cook for a few seconds.

Meanwhile, spread the steaks on both sides with the French mustard, season liberally.

Push the onion mixture to one side and place the steaks in the pan. Cook quickly at first then reduce the heat and cook slowly for about 10 minutes. Remove the steaks on to a serving dish. Add the Worcestershire sauce and tomato purée to the pan, heat and add the chopped parsley. Spoon this mixture over the meat. Serve with a tossed salad.

Serves 2

Boeuf stroganoff

METRIC/IMPERIAL/AMERICAN
0.5 kg/1¼ lb/1¼ lb fillet of beef
50 g/2 oz/¼ cup unsalted butter
100 g/4 oz/1 cup onion, finely chopped
100 g/4 oz/1 cup mushrooms, sliced
150 ml/¼ pint/⅔ cup soured cream
1 tablespoon French mustard
salt and freshly ground pepper
chopped parsley to garnish

Trim the meat and cut into narrow strips. Heat half the butter in a large frying pan, add the onion and cook slowly until just beginning to colour – about 5 minutes. Stir in the mushrooms and cook for about 2 minutes. Remove these on to a plate and keep hot.

Add the remaining butter and half the beef, cook quickly to seal in the juices. Remove to the plate with the mushrooms and onion, keep warm. Add the remaining meat to the pan and cook quickly as before. Return the beef, mushrooms and onion to the pan, stir in most of the soured cream and the French mustard. Season to taste. Reheat and serve immediately with rice or potatoes and a salad or vegetables. Garnish the stroganoff with the remaining soured cream poured down the centre and parsley.

Serves 4

Curried mince

METRIC/IMPERIAL/AMERICAN
0.5 kg/1 lb/1 lb minced beef
100 g/4 oz/1 cup onion, chopped
1–2 tablespoons concentrated curry sauce
1 tablespoon plain flour
1 beef stock cube
300 ml/$\frac{1}{2}$ pint/1$\frac{1}{4}$ cups water
2 teaspoons tomato purée
1 banana, sliced (optional)
25 g/1 oz/3 tablespoons sultanas
1 tablespoon redcurrant jelly or marmalade

Place the minced beef in a saucepan with the onion and cook
gently to extract the fat and seal the meat. Stir in the curry sauce
and flour, cook for 2 minutes. Add the remaining ingredients,
cover and cook slowly, stirring occasionally, for 40 minutes.

Serve with yellow rice, quartered tomatoes, black olives,
redcurrant jelly and salted peanuts.

Serves 4

Mexican mince

METRIC/IMPERIAL/AMERICAN
0.5 kg/1 lb/1 lb minced beef
100 g/4 oz/1 cup onion, chopped
1 tablespoon dried peppers
1 beef stock cube
1 teaspoon chilli sauce
1 (227-g/8-oz/8-oz) can tomatoes
150 ml/$\frac{1}{4}$ pint/$\frac{2}{3}$ cup water
$\frac{1}{2}$ teaspoon paprika
salt and pepper
1 (283-g/10-oz/10-oz) can red kidney beans
1 (64-g/2$\frac{1}{4}$-oz/2$\frac{1}{4}$-oz) packet instant potato
slices of tomato to garnish

Place the minced beef in a saucepan with the onion, heat gently
to extract the fat and seal the meat. Stir in the dried peppers,
crumbled stock cube, chilli sauce, tomatoes, water, paprika
pepper and seasoning to taste. Cover and simmer gently for
45 minutes. Add the drained beans and cook for a further
10 minutes. Place in a heated flameproof serving dish.

Make up the potato according to the packet instructions.
Pipe a border of potato around the edge of the serving dish.
Place under a preheated grill to brown and garnish with the
tomato slices.

Serves 4

Quick shepherd's pie

METRIC/IMPERIAL/AMERICAN
1 (418-g/14¾-oz/14¾-oz) can minced beef with onion
2 tablespoons/2 tablespoons/3 tablespoons plain flour
1 tablespoon tomato purée
1 (64-g/2¼-oz/2¼-oz) packet instant potato
1 small packet potato crisps
GARNISH:
quarters of tomato
parsley sprig

Place the minced beef in a saucepan and heat gently, stirring. Blend the flour with a little water and add to the mince with the tomato purée. Gradually bring to the boil, stirring occasionally.

Meanwhile, make up the instant potato according to packet instructions and crush the crisps in the bag with a rolling pin.

Place the hot mince in a heated flameproof dish, top with piped mashed potato or spoon the potato on and level the surface with a fork. Sprinkle over the crushed crisps. Brown under a hot grill. Serve immediately, garnished with the tomato quarters and parsley.

Serves 4

Beefburgers with tomato sauce

METRIC/IMPERIAL/AMERICAN
0.5 kg/1 lb/1 lb lean minced beef
1 medium onion, finely chopped
½ teaspoon French mustard
½ teaspoon Worcestershire sauce
salt and pepper
½ teaspoon dried mixed herbs
oil for frying
TOMATO SAUCE:
15 g/½ oz/1 tablespoon butter or margarine
1 small onion, chopped
1 (227-g/8-oz/8-oz) can tomatoes
1 tablespoon tomato ketchup

Place the beef in a bowl with the onion, mustard, Worcestershire sauce, seasoning and herbs, mix well. Divide into 8 equal portions and shape into rounds. Fry quickly in the oil to seal, then reduce the heat and cook for about 4 minutes each side. Drain.

Meanwhile, make the sauce by placing the butter or margarine in a small saucepan and adding the onion. Cook for a few minutes then stir in the remaining sauce ingredients. Cook for about 10 minutes until sauce is reduced. Season.

Serve the beefburgers with the tomato sauce.

Serves 4

Corned cabbage sweet and sour

METRIC/IMPERIAL/AMERICAN
25 g/1 oz/2 tablespoons butter or margarine
1 large onion, sliced
0.5 kg/1 lb/1 lb white cabbage
salt and pepper
1 tablespoon water
1 (340-g/12-oz/12-oz) can corned beef
2 tablespoons/2 tablespoons/3 tablespoons vinegar
2 teaspoons demerara sugar
2 tablespoons/2 tablespoons/3 tablespoons mixed pickle
1 teaspoon poppy seeds
parsley sprig to garnish

Melt the butter or margarine in a frying pan, add the onion and fry gently without browning until soft.

Prepare and shred the cabbage, add to the onion with the seasoning and water. Cover the pan and simmer gently, stirring occasionally, for about 10–15 minutes. Place the cabbage in an ovenproof casserole leaving a space in the centre.

Cut the corned beef into slices and arrange in the centre of the casserole. Place the vinegar, sugar and pickle in a small saucepan, heat gently until the sugar dissolves. Pour the sauce over the corned beef, cover with foil and heat in the centre of a moderate oven (180°C, 350°F, Gas Mark 4) for about 20 minutes. Remove the foil. Sprinkle the cabbage with poppy seeds and garnish with a sprig of parsley.

Serves 3–4

Veal with capers

METRIC/IMPERIAL/AMERICAN
4 veal escalopes
seasoned flour
50 g/2 oz/¼ cup butter
juice of ½ lemon
2 tablespoons/2 tablespoons/3 tablespoons capers
GARNISH:
anchovy fillets
chopped parsley
lemon butterflies

If the veal has not been flattened by the butcher, place between 2 pieces of greaseproof paper and flatten with a rolling pin. Coat each piece of veal with the seasoned flour.

Melt the butter in a frying pan and cook the veal very slowly on both sides for about 10 minutes. Remove and keep hot. Add the lemon juice and capers to the pan, heat through and spoon over the veal. Garnish with curled anchovy fillets, capers, chopped parsley and lemon butterflies.

Serves 4

Quick curry

METRIC/IMPERIAL/AMERICAN
1 tablespoon oil
1 small onion, chopped
1 (440-g/15½-oz/16-oz) can mulligatawny soup
2 teaspoons concentrated curry sauce
1 tablespoon tomato ketchup
1 tablespoon cornflour
2 tablespoons/2 tablespoons/3 tablespoons water
25 g/1 oz/3 tablespoons sultanas
350 g/12 oz/12 oz cold cooked meat (beef, lamb, luncheon
    meat or 4 chicken joints)
chopped parsley to garnish

Place the oil in a saucepan, add the onion and sauté gently until
soft. Stir in the soup, curry sauce and tomato ketchup. Blend the
cornflour with the water and add to the pan. Bring to the boil,
stirring, and simmer for about 3 minutes until the cornflour has
thickened. Stir in the sultanas.

If not using chicken joints, cut the meat into cubes. Add the
chicken joints or cubed meat to the saucepan. Heat through
gently for 10–15 minutes. Garnish with chopped parsley.

Serve with chopped green pepper, croûtons of bread and
small savoury biscuits. An accompanying tomato salad may be
served separately.

Serves 4

Sweet and sour lamb kebabs

METRIC/IMPERIAL/AMERICAN
0.75 kg/1½ lb/1½ lb piece of top leg of lamb, boned
8 rashers streaky bacon
2 lambs' kidneys
1 small green pepper
100 g/4 oz/1 cup button mushrooms
12 bay leaves
2 tomatoes, quartered
oil for brushing
225 g/8 oz/generous cup long-grain rice
1 teaspoon turmeric
SWEET AND SOUR SAUCE:
1 tablespoon thick honey
1 tablespoon vinegar
1 (227-g/8-oz/8-oz) jar redcurrant jelly

Cut the meat into 2.5-cm/1-inch cubes. Derind the bacon, cut
each rasher in half and roll up. Skin the kidneys, cut in half and
remove the core. Cut the pepper into bite-size pieces. Thread the
lamb, bacon, kidneys, pepper and mushrooms alternately on to
4 large skewers with the bay leaves and tomatoes. Brush the
kebabs with a little oil and cook under the grill for 15 minutes.

Meanwhile, cook the rice in boiling salted water with the
turmeric for 12–15 minutes. Place the honey, vinegar and
redcurrant jelly in a small saucepan. Bring to the boil and
reduce. Drain the rice and arrange on a serving dish. Place the
kebabs on top. Serve the sauce separately with a tossed salad.

Serves 4   *Illustrated on the cover*

Baked spiced chops

METRIC/IMPERIAL/AMERICAN
6 tablespoons/6 tablespoons/½ cup mango chutney sauce
2 tablespoons/2 tablespoons/3 tablespoons clear honey
1 teaspoon dried mixed herbs
1 tablespoon made mustard
¼ teaspoon curry powder
salt and freshly ground black pepper
8 best end of neck lamb chops
parsley sprigs to garnish

Mix the chutney sauce, honey, herbs, mustard, curry powder and seasonings together.

Place the chops in a shallow roasting tin, spoon over half the sauce and cook in the centre of a moderately hot oven (200°C, 400°F, Gas Mark 6) for about 15 minutes. Turn the chops over, spoon over the remaining sauce and cook for a further 10 minutes. When cooked, drain on kitchen paper to remove excess fat. Serve hot with baked potatoes and tomatoes or cold. Garnish with parsley. These chops are ideal to take on a picnic.

Serves 4 as a main course, or 8 if taken on a picnic

Lamb chops with apple and mint sauce

METRIC/IMPERIAL/AMERICAN
4 loin of lamb chops
40 g/1½ oz/3 tablespoons butter or margarine
100 g/4 oz/1 cup onion, chopped
50 g/2 oz/½ cup cooking apple, peeled and diced
25 g/1 oz/¼ cup plain flour
300 ml/½ pint/1¼ cups milk
1 tablespoon chopped mint
1 teaspoon white wine vinegar
salt and pepper

Thread the lamb chops on to skewers to keep their shape and place under a moderate grill. Cook slowly for about 20 minutes, turning once.

Meanwhile, make the sauce by placing the butter or margarine in a saucepan, add the onion and cook gently without browning for about 10 minutes until soft. Add the apple and cook for a further 5 minutes. Stir in the flour and gradually add the milk, beating well after each addition. Bring to the boil, stirring, reduce the heat and cook for 2 minutes. Stir in the mint, vinegar and seasoning to taste. Serve separately with the chops.

Serves 4

Rich lamb stew

METRIC/IMPERIAL/AMERICAN
1 (1.25-kg/2½-lb/2½-lb) joint top leg of lamb
25 g/1 oz/2 tablespoons butter or margarine
225 g/8 oz/½ lb small onions or shallots, peeled
4 rashers streaky bacon, trimmed and cut in pieces
1 clove garlic, crushed
100 g/4 oz/⅔ cup baby carrots
3 sticks celery, sliced
175 g/6 oz/1½ cups button mushrooms
300 ml/½ pint/1¼ cups red cooking wine
salt and pepper
bay leaf
25 g/1 oz/2 tablespoons softened butter
25 g/1 oz/¼ cup plain flour

Remove the lamb from the bone and cut into cubes. Melt the
butter or margarine in a large saucepan and brown the meat,
turning occasionally. Add the onions and cook gently for about
5 minutes until lightly browned. Add the bacon to the pan with
the garlic, carrots and celery. Cook for about 5 minutes. Add
the mushrooms, wine, seasoning and bay leaf. Bring to the boil,
reduce the heat, cover and simmer for about 40–50 minutes
until the meat is tender.

Blend the softened butter and flour together and add in pieces
to the stew, stirring continuously to blend thoroughly. Reheat
until the stew thickens.

Serves 6

Pork chops with sweet and sour sauce

METRIC/IMPERIAL/AMERICAN
4 pork chops
2 tablespoons/2 tablespoons/3 tablespoons oil
50 g/2 oz/½ cup onion, finely chopped
1 (376-g/13¼-oz/13¼-oz) can crushed pineapple
4 tablespoons/4 tablespoons/⅓ cup vinegar
50 g/2 oz/¼ cup soft brown sugar
1 tablespoon soy sauce
salt
1 tablespoon cornflour
watercress to garnish

Place the pork chops on a grill pan, brush lightly with oil and
cook under a moderate grill for 25 minutes turning once.

Meanwhile, make the sauce. Place 1 tablespoon oil in a small
saucepan, add the onion and cook slowly until soft. Add the
pineapple, vinegar, sugar, soy sauce and salt to taste, simmer for
10 minutes. Blend the cornflour with a little water and hot
sauce, return to the saucepan blending thoroughly. Bring to the
boil and cook for about 3 minutes until the sauce has thickened
and cleared.

Serve the pork chops arranged on a heated serving dish, with
the sauce spooned over the chops. Garnish with watercress.

Serves 4

Peasant pork

METRIC/IMPERIAL/AMERICAN
0.5 kg/1¼ lb/1¼ lb pork fillet
25 g/1 oz/2 tablespoons butter
1 tablespoon corn oil
3 medium onions, sliced
2 cloves garlic, crushed (optional)
350 g/12 oz/¾ lb tomatoes, skinned and quartered
225 g/8 oz/2 cups mushrooms
salt and pepper
1 tablespoon tomato purée
1 teaspoon dried basil
150 ml/¼ pint/⅔ cup soured cream
chopped parsley to garnish

Trim the pork fillet and cut into 2.5-cm/1-inch cubes.

Melt the butter and oil in a large saucepan and fry the pork quickly to lightly brown and seal in the juices. Add the onions, garlic, tomatoes, mushrooms, seasoning, tomato purée and basil. Blend thoroughly. Cover and cook slowly for 30 minutes or until the meat is tender. Stir in the soured cream, garnish with parsley and serve with cooked rice or noodles.

Serves 4

Grilled gammon with marmalade sauce

METRIC/IMPERIAL/AMERICAN
4 medium gammon steaks
corn oil
1 small onion, chopped
4 tablespoons/4 tablespoons/⅓ cup marmalade
2 teaspoons white wine vinegar
2 teaspoons demerara sugar
watercress to garnish

Preheat a moderate grill. Remove the rind from gammon and snip the fat at intervals with a pair of scissors. Place the steaks in a large bowl, cover with boiling water and leave for about 5 minutes. Drain and brush with oil. Place the gammon steaks on the grill rack and cook gently for 10–15 minutes, turning once.

Place the onion in a small saucepan with 1 teaspoon oil, cook without browning for 5 minutes. Stir in the marmalade, vinegar and sugar, heat gently to dissolve. Bring to the boil and reduce to a syrupy sauce.

Place the gammon on a serving dish and pour over the sauce. Garnish with watercress.

Serves 4

Danish pilaff

METRIC/IMPERIAL/AMERICAN
25 g/1 oz/2 tablespoons butter or margarine
1 tablespoon oil
1 medium onion, chopped
2 sticks celery, sliced
175–225 g/6–8 oz/$\frac{1}{2}$ lb forehock bacon steak
225 g/8 oz/generous cup long-grain rice
450–600 ml/$\frac{3}{4}$–1 pint/2–2$\frac{1}{2}$ cups chicken stock
50 g/2 oz/$\frac{1}{3}$ cup sultanas
1 medium green pepper
toasted flaked almonds to garnish

Place the butter and oil in a frying pan, add the onion and celery
and cook slowly until soft – about 10 minutes.

Remove the rind from the bacon and cut into small strips.
Add to the pan and cook slowly, stirring, for about 5 minutes.
Stir in the rice and cook for 2 minutes until the rice is opaque.
Add 450 ml/$\frac{3}{4}$ pint/2 cups of the chicken stock, cook gently,
stirring occasionally, for 20 minutes; add the extra stock if the
rice becomes too dry.

Stir in the sultanas, cut the pepper into strips, removing seeds
and pith, and add to the rice. Cook for a further 10 minutes.
Spoon the pilaff on to a serving dish and sprinkle with the
toasted almonds.

Serves 4

Sausage stew

METRIC/IMPERIAL/AMERICAN
0.5 kg/1 lb/1 lb cocktail sausages or chipolatas, twisted in
    half
25 g/1 oz/2 tablespoons lard
1 large onion, sliced
50 g/2 oz/$\frac{1}{4}$ cup streaky bacon, chopped
25 g/1 oz/$\frac{1}{4}$ cup plain flour
300 ml/$\frac{1}{2}$ pint/1$\frac{1}{4}$ cups beef stock
100 g/4 oz/1 cup button mushrooms, sliced
1 tablespoon tomato purée
salt and pepper
1 (220-g/7$\frac{3}{4}$-oz/8-oz) can baked beans
chopped parsley to garnish

Place the sausages and lard in a saucepan and fry the sausages
very slowly until lightly browned, turning frequently, for about
10 minutes. Remove and keep warm.

Add the onion to the fat, sauté gently until lightly browned.
Add the streaky bacon and cook for 2–3 minutes. Stir in the
flour, add the stock, mushrooms, tomato purée and seasoning.
Blend thoroughly.

Return the sausages to the pan, stir in the baked beans, cover
and cook slowly for 10–15 minutes. Remove to a serving dish
and garnish with parsley. Serve with mashed potato and carrots.

Serves 4

Sausages with lychees

METRIC/IMPERIAL/AMERICAN
0.5 kg/1 lb/1 lb pork chipolata sausages
1 medium onion, sliced
100 g/4 oz/4 oz baby carrots
1 (312-g/11-oz/11-oz) can lychees
2 tablespoons/2 tablespoons/3 tablespoons tomato purée
2 teaspoons soy sauce
salt and pepper

Place the sausages in a frying pan and fry for about 10 minutes, turning frequently, to brown the sausages. Remove from pan and keep hot. Drain off all but 1 tablespoon of fat from the pan, add the onion and carrots and cook gently without browning for about 10 minutes.

Drain the juice from the lychees and add to the pan with the tomato purée, soy sauce and seasoning. Blend thoroughly, return the sausages to the pan and cook for a further 10 minutes.

Stir in the lychees and heat through for a few minutes. Serve with buttered noodles.

Serves 4

Sausage surprise

METRIC/IMPERIAL/AMERICAN
100 g/4 oz/1 cup plain flour
pinch salt
1 egg
300 ml/$\frac{1}{2}$ pint/1$\frac{1}{4}$ cups milk
FILLING :
1 tablespoon corn oil
175 g/6 oz/1$\frac{1}{2}$ cups onion, chopped
0.5 kg/1 lb/1 lb pork chipolata sausages
1 large cooking apple, diced
pinch dried sage
salt and pepper

Place the flour and salt in a bowl. Beat the egg and add to the flour with a little milk, beat well to make a smooth batter. Gradually add the remaining milk. Make 8–10 pancakes in a 20–23-cm/8–9-inch frying pan. Keep warm.

Place the oil in a frying pan, add the onion and cook for about 5 minutes. Remove. Place the sausages in the frying pan and cook for about 10 minutes to evenly brown. Drain off most of the fat. Return the onion to the pan. Add the apple with the sage and seasoning. Cook for about 5 minutes until the apple is pulpy. (A pinch of sugar may be added to slightly sweeten the apple.) Divide the sausages and apple and onion sauce mixture between the pancakes and roll up. Serve hot.

Serves 4

Spicy sausagemeat patties

METRIC/IMPERIAL/AMERICAN
0.5 kg/1 lb/2 cups pork or beef sausagemeat
1 teaspoon dried mixed herbs
1 tablespoon tomato ketchup
½ teaspoon powdered cumin
25 g/1 oz/½ cup fresh breadcrumbs
seasoned flour
oil for frying

Place the sausagemeat in a bowl with the herbs, ketchup, cumin and breadcrumbs, mix evenly. Divide the mixture into 6 portions, using a little of the seasoned flour to shape the mixture into rounds about 1.5 cm/¾ inch thick. Heat a little oil in the frying pan and cook the patties gently for about 6 minutes each side.

Serve either hot or cold in baps, with baked beans and tomato quarters secured on cocktail sticks.

Makes 6

Liver and bacon kebabs

METRIC/IMPERIAL/AMERICAN
350 g/12 oz/¾ lb lamb's liver, in one piece
6 rashers streaky bacon
2 medium onions, quartered
oil for brushing
salt and pepper

Trim the liver and cut into 1-cm/½-inch cubes. Remove the rind from the bacon and 'stretch' each rasher with the back of a knife. Cut each rasher in half and roll up. Thread the liver, bacon and onion alternately on to 4 skewers (as shown in photograph).

Preheat a moderate grill, place the skewers in the grill pan, brush with the oil and season liberally. Place under the grill and cook for 10 minutes, turning frequently and basting with the pan juices when necessary.

Serves 4

Piquant liver with noodles

METRIC/IMPERIAL/AMERICAN
350 g/12 oz/¾ lb lamb's liver
225 g/8 oz/2 cups onion, chopped
1 clove garlic, crushed
75 g/3 oz/6 tablespoons butter or margarine
1 tablespoon dry sherry
salt and pepper
12 pimento-stuffed olives, sliced
1 tablespoon chopped parsley
225 g/8 oz/2 cups noodles
chopped parsley to garnish

Cut the liver into small slices, place in a bowl and cover with boiling water. Leave for about 3 minutes then drain. Place the onion and garlic in a frying pan with 50 g/2 oz/¼ cup of the butter or margarine. Sauté, without browning, until soft. Add the liver and cook for about 5 minutes. Stir in the sherry and seasoning, simmer for a further 5 minutes. Add half of the olives and the parsley.

Meanwhile, cook the noodles in boiling salted water until just tender – about 12 minutes. When tender, drain well and add the remaining butter.

Arrange the noodles in a heated serving dish and pile the liver on top. Garnish with chopped parsley and remaining sliced olives.

Serves 4–5

Veal and chicken liver gratin

METRIC/IMPERIAL/AMERICAN
1 tablespoon oil
40 g/1½ oz/3 tablespoons butter
1 large onion, chopped
0.5 kg/1 lb/1 lb minced veal
225 g/8 oz/½ lb chicken livers, trimmed and chopped
1 tablespoon tomato purée
½ teaspoon dried thyme
salt and pepper
1 tablespoon cornflour
1 kg/2 lb/2 lb potatoes
slices of tomato and parsley sprig to garnish

Place the oil and 15 g/½ oz/1 tablespoon butter in a large saucepan, add the onion and cook for about 10 minutes to soften. Stir in the veal and cook for about 5 minutes, add the chicken livers, tomato puree, thyme and seasoning. Blend the cornflour with 1 tablespoon water, stir into the mixture and cook for about 10 minutes to thicken.

Meanwhile, cut the potatoes in half and cook in boiling salted water until just tender. Cut into slices.

Place layers of the mince and sliced potato in a deep flameproof dish, finishing with a layer of potato. Melt the remaining butter and use to brush over the potato. Place under a preheated grill and cook until the potato is golden. Garnish. Serve with a tossed green salad.

Serves 5

Kidneys in sherry cream sauce

METRIC/IMPERIAL/AMERICAN
175 g/6 oz/1½ cups onion, chopped
25 g/1 oz/2 tablespoons butter or margarine
12 lambs' kidneys
3 tablespoons/3 tablespoons/¼ cup seasoned flour
100 g/4 oz/1 cup mushrooms, quartered
300 ml/½ pint/1¼ cups stock
2 tablespoons/2 tablespoons/3 tablespoons sherry
salt and pepper
150 ml/¼ pint/⅔ cup double cream
chopped parsley to garnish

Sauté the onion gently in a frying pan with the butter or margarine for about 10 minutes.

Meanwhile, remove skin from kidneys, cut in half and remove the core with a pair of scissors. Toss lightly in the seasoned flour. Remove the onion from the pan then add the kidneys. Cook, turning occasionally, for about 5 minutes. Add the onion, mushrooms, stock, sherry and seasoning, simmer for about 15–20 minutes. Spoon into a serving dish and pour over the cream. Garnish with chopped parsley and serve with noodles tossed in butter.

Serves 4

Devilled kidneys

METRIC/IMPERIAL/AMERICAN
25 g/1 oz/2 tablespoons butter or margarine
100 g/4 oz/1 cup onion, chopped
9 lambs' kidneys
1 tablespoon plain flour
150 ml/¼ pint/⅔ cup chicken stock
1 teaspoon brown fruit sauce
¼ teaspoon French mustard
1 tablespoon tomato purée
salt and pepper

Place the butter or margarine and onion in a frying pan and cook gently until lightly browned. Meanwhile, prepare the kidneys by cutting each in half, removing the outer skin and cutting out the core with a pair of scissors. Toss lightly in the flour. Add the kidneys to the pan and fry briskly for about 3 minutes to seal in the juices. Stir in the remaining ingredients. Gradually bring to the boil, stirring gently, and cook for about 10 minutes, stirring occasionally. Place in a serving dish and serve with plain boiled rice or noodles.

Serves 3

Lemon and honey chicken

METRIC/IMPERIAL/AMERICAN
50 g/2 oz/¼ cup butter
4 chicken joints
2 sprigs lemon thyme (if available)
2 tablespoons/2 tablespoons/3 tablespoons chopped
   parsley
4 tablespoons/4 tablespoons/⅓ cup clear honey
juice of 1 lemon
freshly ground black pepper
GARNISH:
lemon slices
parsley sprig

Melt the butter in a frying pan with a lid. Place the chicken joints in the pan and cook until lightly browned all over. Cover and cook gently for about 25 minutes, turning once. Wash and chop the lemon thyme, if used. Add to the chicken with the parsley, honey, lemon juice and pepper. Turn up the heat and baste the chicken with this mixture, cooking for a further 2 minutes.

Place the chicken on a serving dish and keep hot. Reduce the sauce a little over a high heat then spoon over the chicken. Garnish with lemon slices and parsley.

Serves 4

Asparagus chicken suprême

METRIC/IMPERIAL/AMERICAN
4 chicken breasts
1 small carrot, quartered
1 onion, quartered
bouquet garni
salt and pepper
40 g/1½ oz/3 tablespoons butter or margarine
25 g/1 oz/¼ cup plain flour
1 tablespoon dry Vermouth (optional)
1 (283-g/10-oz/10-oz) can asparagus spears
lemon butterflies and slices of stuffed olives to garnish

Carefully remove skin and bone from the chicken breasts, keeping a neat shape. Place in a large shallow pan with a lid. Add the carrot and onion with the bouquet garni and a little seasoning. Pour over enough water to cover. Bring slowly to simmering point, cover and cook slowly for 25–30 minutes until chicken is tender. When the chicken is cooked, remove to a serving dish, cover and keep hot. Reserve 300 ml/½ pint/1¼ cups cooking liquor.

Make the sauce by melting the butter or margarine in a small saucepan, add the flour and cook for 1 minute, stir in the dry Vermouth (if used). Gradually stir in the reserved chicken stock, bring to the boil and cook for about 3 minutes, stirring. Season to taste. Pour the sauce over the chicken breasts to coat. Garnish. Heat the asparagus spears and serve with the chicken.

Serves 4

Barbecued chicken

METRIC/IMPERIAL/AMERICAN
50 g/2 oz/¼ cup butter or margarine
1 medium onion, chopped
1 clove garlic, crushed (optional)
1 (396-g/14-oz/14-oz) can tomatoes
1 tablespoon Worcestershire sauce
salt and pepper
1 tablespoon demerara sugar
4 chicken quarters
oil for brushing
watercress sprigs to garnish

Place the butter or margarine in a small saucepan. Add the onion and garlic and cook until soft, without browning, for about 10 minutes. Stir in the tomatoes, Worcestershire sauce, seasoning and sugar. Stir well, bring to the boil, reduce the heat and simmer for 20 minutes until reduced and thick.

Preheat a moderate grill and place the chicken quarters in a grill pan. Brush the chicken with oil and cook slowly, turning once, for 10 minutes. Remove the chicken from the grill, spoon the sauce over the quarters and continue cooking slowly for a further 15 minutes, turning once. Baste with the remaining sauce during the cooking. Serve hot, garnished with watercress.

Serves 4

Chicken and mushroom casserole

METRIC/IMPERIAL/AMERICAN
4 chicken joints
1 teaspoon paprika pepper
1 teaspoon mustard powder
25 g/1 oz/2 tablespoons butter or margarine
2 teaspoons corn oil
100 g/4 oz/1 cup onion, chopped
225 g/8 oz/2 cups button mushrooms, sliced
1 (396-g/14-oz/14-oz) can tomatoes
2 teaspoons chicken stock powder
salt and pepper

Coat the chicken joints with the paprika pepper and mustard. Melt the butter and oil in a frying pan and cook the chicken gently to seal and lightly brown it — about 5–10 minutes. Remove from the pan. Add the onion and cook for about 5 minutes. Add the mushrooms, tomatoes and chicken stock powder. Season to taste. Bring to the boil and return the chicken to the pan. Cover and simmer gently for 25 minutes until the chicken is tender.

Serves 4

Vegetable dishes and salads

These dishes can either be served on their own as a lunch or supper snack or may be the accompanying vegetable to a main meal. The salad ideas are particularly inspired without taking hours of preparation.

Courgette and tomato grill

METRIC/IMPERIAL/AMERICAN
1 medium onion
0.5 kg/1 lb/1 lb courgettes
50 g/2 oz/¼ cup butter or margarine
1 (396-g/14-oz/14-oz) can tomatoes or use fresh tomatoes
1 teaspoon dried marjoram
salt and pepper
50 g/2 oz/½ cup Cheddar cheese, grated
2 tablespoons/2 tablespoons/3 tablespoons browned breadcrumbs
chopped parsley to garnish

Slice the onion. Wash the courgettes, trim off the ends and cut into 0.5-cm/¼-inch slices.

Melt the butter or margarine in a large pan, add the onion, courgettes, tomatoes, marjoram and seasoning. Cover and simmer gently for 30 minutes, stirring frequently.

Preheat a medium grill. Turn the vegetables into a flameproof dish, mix the cheese and breadcrumbs together and sprinkle over the top. Place under the grill for about 5 minutes until the cheese is melted and lightly browned. Garnish with chopped parsley.

Serves 4

Celery gratin

METRIC/IMPERIAL/AMERICAN
1 (0.5-kg/1-lb 2-oz/1-lb 2-oz) can celery hearts
4 slices ham
75 g/3 oz/¾ cup onion, chopped
40 g/1½ oz/3 tablespoons butter or margarine
40 g/1½ oz/6 tablespoons plain flour
450 ml/¾ pint/2 cups milk
salt and pepper
50 g/2 oz/½ cup Cheddar cheese, grated
25 g/1 oz/½ cup fresh white breadcrumbs
parsley sprigs to garnish

Drain the celery hearts well and wrap the ham slices around
them. Place in an ovenproof dish.

Place the onion in a saucepan with the butter or margarine
and sauté gently until soft – about 5 minutes. Stir in the flour,
cook for 1 minute then gradually add the milk. Bring to the
boil, stirring, and cook for 2 minutes. Add seasoning to taste.
Pour the sauce over the celery. Mix the cheese and breadcrumbs
together and sprinkle over the sauce. Bake in a moderately hot
oven (200°C, 400°F, Gas Mark 6) for 20–25 minutes until the
topping is crisp and golden. Garnish with parsley.

Serves 4

Savoury cauliflower

METRIC/IMPERIAL/AMERICAN
1 kg/2 lb/2 lb cauliflower
1 medium onion
25 g/1 oz/2 tablespoons butter or margarine
100 g/4 oz/¼ lb streaky bacon, derinded and chopped
100 g/4 oz/1 cup mushrooms, chopped
salt and pepper
40 g/1½ oz/3 tablespoons butter or margarine
25 g/1 oz/¼ cup plain flour
150 ml/¼ pint/⅔ cup milk
25 g/1 oz/¼ cup Parmesan cheese, grated
1 tablespoon browned breadcrumbs

Prepare the cauliflower and break into sprigs or leave whole.
Cook in boiling salted water until just crisp – about 15 minutes.
Drain, reserving 150 ml/¼ pint/⅔ cup of the cooking liquor.

Chop the onion, place in a pan with the butter and cook until
soft. Add the bacon and mushrooms and cook for about 5
minutes, add seasoning. Spread over the base of an ovenproof
dish and place the cauliflower on top.

Prepare the sauce by melting the butter or margarine in a
small pan. Add the flour, stirring, cook for 1 minute then
gradually stir in the milk and cauliflower liquor. Bring to the
boil, stirring, cook for 2 minutes. Pour over the cauliflower.
Mix the cheese and breadcrumbs together, sprinkle over the
cauliflower and place under the grill to heat through.

Serves 4

Piquant spaghetti

METRIC/IMPERIAL/AMERICAN
225 g/8 oz/½ lb spaghetti
25 g/1 oz/2 tablespoons butter or margarine
175 g/6 oz/1½ cups onion, chopped
25 g/1 oz/¼ cup plain flour
1 teaspoon dry mustard
1 (396-g/14-oz/14-oz) can tomatoes
150 ml/¼ pint/⅔ cup chicken stock
1 tablespoon tomato purée
1 tablespoon vinegar
1 tablespoon Worcestershire sauce
pinch sugar
salt and pepper
1 tablespoon chopped parsley
1 teaspoon dried oregano
grated Parmesan cheese
chopped parsley

Cook the spaghetti in boiling salted water until tender. Drain.
   Meanwhile, melt the butter or margarine in a saucepan, add the onion and sauté until soft. Stir in the flour and mustard and cook for 1 minute. Add the tomatoes, chicken stock, tomato purée, vinegar, Worcestershire sauce, sugar, seasoning, parsley and oregano. Bring to the boil, simmer for 10 minutes. Place the spaghetti on a serving plate or plates. Pour the sauce in the centre and serve sprinkled with Parmesan and parsley.

Serves 4

Stuffed marrow rings

METRIC/IMPERIAL/AMERICAN
1 medium marrow, peeled, deseeded and cut into 3.5-cm/1½-inch rings
2 tablespoons/2 tablespoons/3 tablespoons corn oil
225 g/8 oz/2 cups onion, chopped
2 cloves garlic, crushed
0.5 kg/1 lb/1 lb tomatoes, skinned and chopped
75 g/3 oz/1½ cups fresh breadcrumbs
2 tablespoons/2 tablespoons/3 tablespoons chopped parsley
1 teaspoon dried mixed herbs
100 g/4 oz/¼ lb aubergine, chopped
salt and pepper
25 g/1 oz/¼ cup Parmesan cheese, grated
watercress sprig to garnish

Cook the marrow in boiling salted water until just tender – about 5–10 minutes. Drain well and arrange these rings in a large ovenproof dish.
   Place the oil, onion and garlic in a frying pan and sauté for about 10 minutes until soft. Add the tomatoes, breadcrumbs, parsley, mixed herbs, aubergine and seasoning, blend thoroughly and cook for about 5 minutes.
   Divide the mixture between the marrow rings, sprinkle each with a little cheese. Place under a moderate grill to lightly brown the cheese and heat through. Garnish with the watercress.

Serves 3–4

Vegetable pancakes

METRIC/IMPERIAL/AMERICAN
50 g/2 oz/¼ cup butter or margarine
225 g/8 oz/½ lb onions, finely sliced
175 g/6 oz/1½ cups mushrooms, chopped
350 g/12 oz/¾ lb tomatoes, skinned and chopped
50 g/2 oz/1 cup fresh brown breadcrumbs
½ teaspoon garlic salt
½ teaspoon paprika pepper
50 g/2 oz/½ cup shelled Brazil nuts, sliced
PANCAKE BATTER:
125 g/4 oz/1 cup plain flour
salt
1 large egg
1 tablespoon oil
300 ml/½ pint/1¼ cups milk

Melt the butter or margarine in a frying pan, add the onion and cook for about 10 minutes until soft. Stir in the mushrooms, tomatoes, breadcrumbs, salt, paprika and nuts. Keep warm.

Sift the flour and salt into a bowl, make a well in the centre. Break in the egg and oil, then gradually add the milk. Grease a 20–23-cm/8–9-inch frying pan and pour in just enough batter to cover the pan. Cook 8 pancakes lightly on both sides.

Fold the pancakes into four and fill each with the stuffing. Place on a serving dish and garnish with watercress. Mix 150 ml/¼ pint/⅔ cup soured cream, 1 tablespoon tomato puree and ⅓ teaspoon dried herbs. Serve this sauce separately.

Serves 4

Vegetable risotto

METRIC/IMPERIAL/AMERICAN
2 tablespoons/2 tablespoons/3 tablespoons corn oil
100 g/4 oz/1 cup onion, sliced
2 carrots, diced
15 g/½ oz/1 tablespoon dried peppers
1 tablespoon vegetable extract
1 litre/1¾ pints/4¼ cups boiling water
175 g/6 oz/scant cup long-grain rice
2 tablespoons/2 tablespoons/3 tablespoons tomato purée
25 g/1 oz/3 tablespoons sultanas
1 (113-g/4-oz/¼-lb) packet frozen peas
grated cheese to garnish

Place the oil in a frying pan, add the onion and saute gently for about 5 minutes. Add the carrots and cook for a further 5 minutes. Stir in the dried peppers, vegetable extract and boiling water. Add the rice, tomato puree and sultanas. Cook for about 20 minutes, stirring occasionally. Add a little more water if necessary. Stir in the peas and cook for about 10 minutes.

Serve immediately sprinkled with grated cheese.

Serves 4

Mixed vegetable pasta

METRIC/IMPERIAL/AMERICAN
225 g/8 oz/½ lb macaroni
225 g/8 oz/½ lb frozen mixed vegetables, thawed
3 large tomatoes, skinned and chopped
1 (298-g/10½-oz/10½-oz) can condensed mushroom soup
1 tablespoon vegetable extract (optional)
croûtons of toast to garnish

Cook the macaroni in boiling salted water for about 8 minutes, then add the thawed mixed vegetables and cook for about 5 minutes. Drain well. Add the chopped tomatoes.

Heat the soup in a saucepan, stir in the pasta, vegetables, vegetable extract, if used, and heat for about 5 minutes.

Place in a heated serving dish and serve with croutons of toast.

Serves 4

Parsnip fritters

METRIC/IMPERIAL/AMERICAN
0.5 kg/1 lb/1 lb parsnips
50 g/2 oz/½ cup plain flour
salt
2 teaspoons cornflour
1 tablespoon oil
4 tablespoons/4 tablespoons/⅓ cup tepid water
1 egg white
oil for frying
grated cheese to garnish (optional)

Prepare the parsnips and cut into quarters lengthways. Cook in boiling salted water until tender.

To make the batter, sift the flour, salt and cornflour into a bowl. Make a well in the centre and add the oil and water gradually, beating well to give a smooth consistency. Allow the batter to stand while cooking the parsnips.

Drain the parsnips well on kitchen paper. Whisk the egg white until stiff and dry, and fold into the batter mixture until thoroughly incorporated. Heat a pan of oil until a piece of bread turns golden in about 20 seconds.

Dip some of the parsnip pieces into the batter. Drain off any excess batter and fry carefully in the oil for about 4 minutes. Drain on kitchen paper. Repeat in batches until all the parsnips have been fried.

Serve sprinkled with grated cheese, if liked.

Serves 2–3

Baked stuffed tomatoes

METRIC/IMPERIAL/AMERICAN
12 large tomatoes
75 g/3 oz/6 tablespoons butter or margarine
1 medium onion, chopped
50 g/2 oz/½ cup button mushrooms
100 g/4 oz/¼ lb ham
75 g/3 oz/⅔ cup cooked rice
½ teaspoon dried basil
salt and pepper
mustard and cress to garnish

Wash and dry the tomatoes, cut a slice off from the stalk end for the lid. Using a teaspoon, scoop out the flesh from each tomato.

Place the butter or margarine in a saucepan with the onion and fry gently until soft. Finely chop the mushrooms and ham and add to the cooked onion with the rice, basil and seasoning to taste. Add the flesh from the tomatoes. Cook for a few minutes to reduce the liquid from the tomatoes, stirring occasionally so that the rice does not stick to the base of the pan.

Using a teaspoon, fill the tomato shells with this mixture. Place in an ovenproof dish, top each with a tomato lid and bake on the top shelf of a moderate oven (180°C, 350°F, Gas Mark 4) for about 20 minutes.

Serve hot with French bread and garnish with mustard and cress.

Serves 4

Leek and orange salad

METRIC/IMPERIAL/AMERICAN
2 medium leeks
3 large tomatoes
1 large orange
salt and pepper
mustard powder
castor sugar
2 tablespoons/2 tablespoons/3 tablespoons corn oil
1 tablespoon vinegar

Prepare the leeks by cutting off some of the green foliage and the root. Thinly slice and wash very thoroughly to remove all grit. Place in a bowl. Remove the skin from the tomatoes by immersing in boiling water, leave for a few seconds, then peel off the skin. Cut the tomatoes in quarters and scoop out the seeds, then add to the leeks.

Using a sharp knife, peel off the rind and pith from the orange and cut in between the membranes to remove the segments. Add to the leek and tomato mixture.

Place the seasonings and sugar in a small bowl. Blend in the corn oil and then mix in the vinegar. Pour over the salad.

Serves 4

Ham and pasta salad

METRIC/IMPERIAL/AMERICAN
100 g/4 oz/1 cup pasta shells
1 (284-g/10-oz/10-oz) can cut green beans or use frozen
50 g/2 oz/½ cup button mushrooms
1–2 cloves garlic, crushed
salt and pepper
pinch mustard powder
pinch castor sugar
3 tablespoons/3 tablespoons/¼ cup corn oil
2 tablespoons/2 tablespoons/3 tablespoons vinegar
2 canned red peppers
2 slices cooked lean ham

Cook the pasta in boiling salted water for about 20 minutes until just tender. Drain well and place on kitchen paper.

If using frozen beans, cook according to the directions on the packet, drain and refresh under cold water. Slice the mushrooms.

Place the garlic, seasonings and sugar in a salad bowl, blend in the oil and gradually beat in the vinegar. Add the pasta, beans and mushrooms to the dressing. Drain the red peppers well, cut into dice and add to the mixture. Remove any excess fat from the ham and cut into strips. Add to the bowl and blend until all the ingredients are evenly coated in the dressing. Serve with French bread.

Serves 4

Spinach and avocado salad

METRIC/IMPERIAL/AMERICAN
100 g/4 oz/¼ lb streaky bacon
salt and pepper
pinch mustard powder
pinch castor sugar
1 clove garlic, crushed
4 tablespoons/4 tablespoons/⅓ cup oil
2 tablespoons/2 tablespoons/3 tablespoons lemon juice
350 g/12 oz/¾ lb fresh spinach
1 ripe avocado pear
1 small onion, thinly sliced
chopped parsley to garnish (optional)

Derind the bacon, cut into small pieces and fry gently until crisp and lightly browned. Remove and drain on kitchen paper.

Place the seasonings and sugar in a salad bowl and mix in the garlic and oil. Gradually add the lemon juice and beat well.

Remove any thick stalks from the spinach and wash thoroughly several times in fresh water to remove any grit or sand. Shake well to remove excess water and dry in a clean tea towel. Tear into small pieces and add to the dressing with the crispy bacon. Toss to coat in the dressing.

Halve the avocado pear and remove the stone. Peel off the tough outer skin and cut the flesh into bite-sized pieces. Add to the salad and stir round lightly. Sprinkle the top with the sliced onion. Garnish with a little chopped parsley if liked. Serve with French bread.

Serves 4

Malayan curried salad

METRIC/IMPERIAL/AMERICAN
100 g/4 oz/generous ½ cup long-grain rice
150 ml/¼ pint/⅔ cup mayonnaise
1–2 teaspoons concentrated curry sauce
1 (226-g/8-oz/8-oz) can pineapple slices
1 small green pepper, diced
225 g/8 oz/1 cup cooked chicken, diced
25 g/1 oz/3 tablespoons seedless raisins
chopped green pepper to garnish

Cook the rice in boiling salted water for 12–15 minutes until tender. Drain well and spread on kitchen paper to cool.

Place the mayonnaise in a bowl and stir in the curry sauce. Drain the pineapple, dry on kitchen paper and cut into small pieces. Add the green pepper, pineapple, chicken and raisins to the mayonnaise and stir to coat evenly.

Place the rice on a serving dish and top with the curried chicken mixture. Garnish with chopped green pepper.

Serves 3–4

Crunchy bacon salad

METRIC/IMPERIAL/AMERICAN
4 slices white bread, cut 1 cm/½ inch thick
50 g/2 oz/¼ cup butter or margarine
5 tablespoons/5 tablespoons/6 tablespoons oil
8 rashers streaky bacon
225 g/8 oz/2 cups button mushrooms, thickly sliced
½ small onion
salt and pepper
pinch dry mustard
1 tablespoon vinegar
50 g/2 oz/⅓ cup pimento-stuffed olives, sliced
2 tablespoons/2 tablespoons/3 tablespoons chopped
   parsley

Remove the crusts and cut the bread into large cubes. Melt the butter or margarine in a frying pan with 2 tablespoons/2 tablespoons/3 tablespoons of the oil. Heat gently and fry the bread cubes, turning frequently, until crisp and golden. Remove and drain on kitchen paper.

Remove the rind from the bacon and cut into large pieces. Fry until slightly crisp. Remove from the pan and drain well. Add the mushrooms to the pan and fry slowly until just soft. Remove, drain and place in a salad bowl.

Grate the onion and add to the mushrooms with the seasoning and mustard. Blend the remaining oil and vinegar into mushroom mixture. Cool and add remaining ingredients.

Serves 4

Cheese, apple and nut coleslaw

METRIC/IMPERIAL/AMERICAN
0.5 kg/1 lb/1 lb firm white cabbage
100 g/4 oz/1 cup red Leicester cheese, grated or crumbled
100 g/4 oz/1 cup onion, finely chopped
1 red eating apple
50 g/2 oz/⅓ cup salted peanuts
4 tablespoons/4 tablespoons/⅓ cup salad cream
salt and pepper
GARNISH:
parsley sprig
sliced pimento-stuffed olives

Shred the cabbage, discarding any tough stalks, and place in a large bowl. Add the cheese and the onion.

Cut the apple into quarters, remove the core and chop or slice. Add to the cabbage mixture with the remaining ingredients, blending well. Season to taste. Garnish with the parsley sprig and sliced stuffed olives. To make this dish more filling, serve with jacket potatoes.

Serves 6

Salami and rice salad

METRIC/IMPERIAL/AMERICAN
75 g/3 oz/scant ½ cup long-grain rice
salt and pepper
pinch dry mustard
pinch castor sugar
3 tablespoons/3 tablespoons/¼ cup oil
1 tablespoon wine vinegar
25 g/1 oz/3 tablespoons currants
1 dill cucumber
1 (198-g/7-oz/7-oz) can sweetcorn with peppers
175 g/6 oz/6 oz Danish salami, cut into strips

Cook the rice in boiling salted water until tender – about 12–15 minutes. Drain and cool.

Place the seasonings and sugar in a bowl, blend in the oil and gradually beat in the vinegar. Add the currants. Chop the cucumber, drain the sweetcorn and add to the dressing with the rice and half the salami. Blend thoroughly. Arrange the remaining salami in a lattice pattern on top.

Serves 4

44

Sweets

To complete the meal most people like to have a sweet dish and a look through the recipes in this section will convince you that speedy desserts are possible. Make use of store cupboard ingredients such as canned fruit and present them as shown in these mouthwatering pictures.

Pineapple and ginger creams

METRIC/IMPERIAL/AMERICAN
1 (226-g/8-oz/8-oz) can pineapple slices
100 g/4 oz/$\frac{1}{4}$ lb gingernut biscuits
2 tablespoons/2 tablespoons/3 tablespoons dry sherry
300 ml/$\frac{1}{2}$ pint/1$\frac{1}{4}$ cups double cream
grated chocolate to decorate

Drain the pineapple well and chop into small pieces. Crush the gingernut biscuits with a rolling pin and mix in the sherry.

Whisk the double cream until lightly whipped and gently fold in the crushed biscuits and pineapple. Spoon into individual glasses and sprinkle with the grated chocolate.

Serves 4–6

Mixed berry salad

METRIC/IMPERIAL/AMERICAN
225 g/8 oz/2 cups blackcurrants
150 ml/¼ pint/⅔ cup sweet white wine
150 ml/¼ pint/⅔ cup water
100 g/4 oz/1 cup icing sugar
3 teaspoons arrowroot
225 g/8 oz/1½ cups strawberries
225 g/8 oz/1½ cups raspberries

Place the blackcurrants in a pan with the wine, water and the icing sugar. Heat gently to dissolve the sugar and soften the fruit – about 10 minutes. Sieve the cooked fruit and allow to cool. Blend the arrowroot with a little water and some of the fruit purée and place in a saucepan with the remaining purée. Bring to the boil, stirring, and cook for about 3 minutes until the mixture thickens and clears. Allow to cool.

Place the remaining prepared fruit in a serving dish, pour over the cooled, thickened sauce. Serve with crisp biscuits or wafers.

Note: This would also be delicious served with ice cream or meringues.

Serves 4–6

Apricot soufflé omelette

METRIC/IMPERIAL/AMERICAN
25 g/1 oz/2 tablespoons butter
1 heaped tablespoon apricot jam
225 g/8 oz/½ lb fresh apricots or use dried
25 g/1 oz/2 tablespoons castor sugar
OMELETTE:
2 eggs
25 g/1 oz/2 tablespoons castor sugar
1 teaspoon cornflour
½ teaspoon vanilla essence

Place the butter and jam in a small saucepan. Heat until just melted. Meanwhile, wash and halve the apricots removing the stones, add to the melted butter and jam. (Soak dried apricots.) Cover and cook very gently for about 5–10 minutes until soft, shaking the saucepan occasionally. Stir in the sugar.

To make the omelette, separate the yolks from the whites and place in separate bowls. Stir the sugar, cornflour and vanilla essence into the yolks. Cream together until thick and pale. Whisk the egg whites until stiff. Fold the whites into the yolk mixture using a metal spoon.

Butter a 25-cm/10-inch frying pan, heat gently. Pour the egg mixture into the pan and cook slowly until the sides are beginning to set. Place the pan under a moderate grill to lightly brown the surface. Spoon the apricot filling on to the centre of the omelette and fold over. Sprinkle with sugar.

Serves 2

Orange and lychee compote

METRIC/IMPERIAL/AMERICAN
2 medium oranges
1 (312-g/11-oz/11-oz) can lychees
2 teaspoons arrowroot
15 g/½ oz/1 tablespoon seedless raisins

Finely grate the rind from one of the oranges and reserve.

Using a sharp knife, cut off the rind and pith from the oranges. Cut out the orange segments from in between the membranes.

Drain the juice from the lychees into a small saucepan. Squeeze any remaining juice from the orange membrane and add to the pan with the grated orange rind.

Blend a little of the juice with the arrowroot, add to the pan and bring to the boil, stirring. Cook for a few seconds until the mixture thickens and clears. Stir in the raisins, lychees and orange segments. Allow to chill before serving.
Note: This compote would make a delicious sauce to serve with ice cream.

Serves 4

Baked bananas and oranges

METRIC/IMPERIAL/AMERICAN
2 large oranges
50 g/2 oz/¼ cup demerara sugar
6 bananas
juice of ½ lemon
25 g/1 oz/2 tablespoons butter
brandy, rum or Grand Marnier (optional)

Grate the rind from one orange and mix with 40 g/1½ oz/3 tablespoons of the sugar. Grate the rind from the other orange and reserve for decoration. Using a sharp knife, remove the pith from the oranges and cut out the segments from in between the membranes. Peel the bananas and cut diagonally into slices. Arrange in alternate layers in an ovenproof dish sprinkling the sugar mixture between each layer. Pour over the lemon juice. Sprinkle the top layer with the remaining sugar and dot with the butter.

Bake for 20 minutes on the centre shelf of a moderately hot oven (190°C, 375°F, Gas Mark 5). Sprinkle with either brandy, rum or Grand Marnier, if liked. Decorate with the grated orange rind and serve with almond twirls.

Serves 4

Fritter quickie

METRIC/IMPERIAL/AMERICAN
8 slices bread, cut 1 cm/½ inch thick
3 large eggs
2 tablespoons/2 tablespoons/3 tablespoons milk
75 g/3 oz/6 tablespoons unsalted butter
apricot jam, warmed

Remove the crusts from the bread. Break the eggs into a large shallow dish. Add the milk and beat with a fork. Quickly dip each side of the bread into the beaten egg and leave to drain on a plate. Melt the butter in a large frying pan and quickly fry the bread slices on both sides for about 3–4 minutes. Keep these hot while cooking the remaining slices. Spread each with the warmed apricot jam and serve immediately.

Serves 4

Banana boats

METRIC/IMPERIAL/AMERICAN
75 g/3 oz/6 tablespoons sugar
25 g/1 oz/¼ cup cocoa powder
300 ml/½ pint/1¼ cups water
few drops vanilla essence
2 frozen chocolate eclairs, thawed
4 bananas

Blend the sugar and cocoa powder with the water. Place in a saucepan and bring slowly to the boil, stirring, until the sugar dissolves. Boil rapidly for about 5 minutes or until the sauce is reduced by half. Add the vanilla essence and allow the sauce to become cold.

Cut the eclairs in half lengthways and place on individual plates. Peel the bananas and place a banana on each eclair half. Spoon chocolate sauce over the bananas.

Note: If liked, halve an ice-cream wafer and stick in the top to represent a sail. Four eclairs may be used, with a banana placed inside each eclair.

Serves 4

Rhubarb surprise

METRIC/IMPERIAL/AMERICAN
0.75 kg/1½ lb/1½ lb fresh rhubarb
6 tablespoons/6 tablespoons/½ cup water
6 tablespoons/6 tablespoons/½ cup redcurrant jelly
grated rind of 1 orange
2 tablespoons/2 tablespoons/3 tablespoons cornflour
1 egg white
150 ml/¼ pint/⅔ cup double cream
crisp biscuits (optional)

Trim the rhubarb and wash thoroughly. Cut into 5-cm/2-inch pieces. Place in a saucepan with 4 tablespoons/4 tablespoons/ ⅓ cup of the water. Bring slowly to the boil and simmer gently for about 10 minutes until the fruit is soft. Stir in the redcurrant jelly and grated orange rind, and simmer uncovered for about 5 minutes until the fruit is pulpy. Blend the cornflour with the remaining water, add some of the hot liquid from the rhubarb and return to the pan. Blend thoroughly, bring to the boil and cook for about 2 minutes until the rhubarb mixture has thickened and the cornflour has cleared. Leave to become cold.

Divide the rhubarb between 6 sundae glasses. Whisk the egg white until stiff and dry. In a separate bowl, whisk the cream until it stands in soft peaks then fold in the egg white. Top each glass with a swirl of cream. Serve with crisp biscuits, if liked.

Serves 6

Butterscotch pears

METRIC/IMPERIAL/AMERICAN
4 ripe pears
juice of 2 lemons
25 g/1 oz/2 tablespoons butter
225 g/8 oz/1 cup soft brown sugar

Peel the pears keeping the stalk intact.

Place the lemon juice, butter and sugar in a saucepan, heat gently to dissolve. Stand the pears in the pan and cook very slowly until just tender, about 10–15 minutes depending on the ripeness of the pears. When tender, remove the pears and boil the sauce until it is thick.

Reduce the heat, return the pears to the pan and baste them with the sauce (taking care, as the sauce is extremely hot, to hold the pears by the stalk). When the pears are evenly coated, place in individual dishes and pour over the remaining sauce.

Serves 4

Chocolate brandy whip

METRIC/IMPERIAL/AMERICAN
75 g/3 oz/3 oz plain chocolate
3 eggs
few drops vanilla essence
1 teaspoon hot water
1 tablespoon brandy
15 g/½ oz/1 tablespoon butter
GARNISH:
whipped cream
grated chocolate (optional)

Melt the chocolate in a bowl over a pan of hot water. Separate the yolks from the whites of the eggs. Beat each egg yolk separately and add one by one to the chocolate, beating well between each addition. Beat in the vanilla essence, water, brandy and gradually add the butter in small pieces, blending thoroughly. Remove the bowl from the heat and allow the chocolate mixture to cool.

When cooled, whisk the egg whites until stiff and carefully fold into the chocolate mixture.

Divide between 4 individual dishes and leave to chill in the refrigerator. Top each with a swirl of cream and a little extra grated chocolate, if liked.

Note: Substitute 1 tablespoon rum for the brandy, if preferred.

Serves 4

Quick chocolate trifle

METRIC/IMPERIAL/AMERICAN
1 jam Swiss roll
1 (212-g/7½-oz/8-oz) can sliced pears, diced
375 ml/13 fl oz/1⅔ cups milk
4 teaspoons custard powder
1 tablespoon cocoa powder
2 teaspoons castor sugar
150 ml/¼ pint/⅔ cup double cream
DECORATION:
glacé cherries
angelica

Cut the Swiss roll into slices and use to line the sides and base of a glass serving dish. Pour over the juice from the canned pears and cover with the diced fruit.

Place most of the milk in a saucepan and bring almost to the boil; blend the remaining milk with the custard and cocoa powder. Stir the hot milk on to the mixture, blend thoroughly and return to the saucepan. Bring to the boil, stirring, and cook for 2–3 minutes until thickened. Stir in the sugar. Allow to cool slightly. Pour the custard over the fruit. Cool.

Pour a little cream over the surface of the trifle then whip the remainder and pipe around the edge. Decorate with glacé cherries and angelica.

Serves 4–5

Lemon tutti-frutti

METRIC/IMPERIAL/AMERICAN

1 (255-g/9-oz/9-oz) packet frozen lemon mousse, thawed
150 ml/¼ pint/⅔ cup double cream
2 tablespoons/2 tablespoons/3 tablespoons lemon curd
25 g/1 oz/3 tablespoons sultanas, chopped
25 g/1 oz/3 tablespoons dried mixed peel
1 tablespoon Grand Marnier or Curaçao

Place the thawed mousse in a bowl, beat gently with a fork to make smooth. Whisk the cream until it stands in soft peaks and stir into the mousse with the remaining ingredients. Spoon into individual glasses and serve slightly chilled with russe biscuits.

Serves 4

Mandarin crunch

METRIC/IMPERIAL/AMERICAN

BASE:

1 (312-g/11-oz/11-oz) can mandarin oranges
100 g/4 oz/½ cup cottage cheese
grated rind of 1 orange

TOPPING:

50 g/2 oz/¼ cup butter
50 g/2 oz/¼ cup demerara sugar
75 g/3 oz/1 cup porridge oats

Drain the juice from the mandarins. Place the cottage cheese in a bowl and stir in the mandarins and orange rind. Divide between 4 individual flameproof dishes or use one large dish.

Melt the butter and sugar together, stir in the porridge oats and mix well. Divide between the dishes or dish and smooth the surface. Place under a hot grill to brown the surface. Serve immediately.

Serves 4

Egg and cheese dishes

When a quick meal is called for everyone thinks of eggs and cheese which do make nutritious, quick meals. By looking through these recipes you will see that the scope is wider than omelettes and egg on toast – both eggs and cheese go well with all kinds of pasta. For freezer owners, quick meals are no problem as pastry cases for delicious savoury flans can be partly baked and frozen in advance, and when required a tasty filling added.

Spaghetti eggs

METRIC/IMPERIAL/AMERICAN
175 g/6 oz/6 oz spaghetti
40 g/1½ oz/3 tablespoons butter
40 g/1½ oz/6 tablespoons plain flour
300 ml/½ pint/1¼ cups milk
175 g/6 oz/1½ cups Cheddar cheese, grated
2 teaspoons grated onion
4 large eggs, hard-boiled
2 tablespoons/2 tablespoons/3 tablespoons dried
  breadcrumbs
2 large tomatoes

Bring a large pan of salted water to the boil. Break the spaghetti into convenient lengths for serving, add to the water and cook for about 8 minutes. When cooked, drain, reserving 150 ml/¼ pint/⅔ cup of the liquor.

Melt the butter in a pan, add the flour and cook for 1 minute. Gradually stir in the milk and reserved cooking liquor. Bring to the boil, stirring, and simmer for 2 minutes. Add most of the cheese, the onion and salt and pepper to taste.

Preheat a moderately hot grill. Place half the spaghetti in a shallow flameproof casserole. Halve the eggs and arrange on the spaghetti. Cover with half the cheese sauce, top with the remaining spaghetti and cover this with the remainder of the cheese sauce. Mix the rest of the cheese and the breadcrumbs together and sprinkle over the top. Slice the tomatoes and arrange around the edge of the dish. Grill for 10 minutes.

Serves 4

Macaroni cheese

METRIC/IMPERIAL/AMERICAN
175 g/6 oz/6 oz cut macaroni
100 g/4 oz/1 cup onion, chopped
1 clove garlic, crushed (optional)
50 g/2 oz/¼ cup butter or margarine
40 g/1½ oz/6 tablespoons plain flour
450 ml/¾ pint/2 cups milk
175 g/6 oz/1½ cups strong Cheddar cheese, grated
salt and pepper
slices of red pepper to garnish

Cook the macaroni in boiling salted water for about 8–10 minutes or until tender. Drain well.

Meanwhile, gently cook the onion and garlic in the butter or margarine until soft. Stir in the flour, cook for 1 minute then gradually blend in the milk. Bring to the boil, stirring, and cook for 3 minutes. Stir in 150 g/5 oz/1¼ cups of the cheese and cook gently for 3 minutes. Add seasoning.

Add the macaroni to the sauce then pour into a flameproof dish. Sprinkle with the remaining cheese and brown under a preheated grill. Garnish with slices of red pepper and serve with sliced green beans or a tossed green salad.

Serves 4–6

Savoury omelette

METRIC/IMPERIAL/AMERICAN
40 g/1½ oz/3 tablespoons butter or margarine
1 medium onion, chopped
225 g/8 oz/½ lb potatoes, peeled and diced
50 g/2 oz/½ cup button mushrooms, sliced
4 large eggs
6 tablespoons/6 tablespoons/½ cup milk
salt and pepper
½ teaspoon dried thyme
2 canned red peppers

Melt the butter or margarine in a large omelette pan. Add the onion and potato, and cook gently for about 10–15 minutes until the potato is just soft. Stir in the mushrooms and cook for 2 minutes.

Break the eggs into a bowl, add the milk, seasoning and herb and whisk together. Drain and chop the red peppers. Add to the egg mixture and pour over the ingredients in the frying pan. Cook gently until lightly browned underneath. Preheat a moderate grill. Place the omelette under the grill and cook the top until lightly browned. Serve hot or cold.

Serves 2–3

Spanish scramble

METRIC/IMPERIAL/AMERICAN
50 g/2 oz/¼ cup unsalted butter
1 medium onion, chopped
½ small green pepper, deseeded and diced
3 large eggs
4 large tomatoes, skinned and deseeded
100 g/4 oz/¼ lb luncheon meat, diced
salt and black pepper

Melt the butter in a pan, add the onion and cook gently for
about 5 minutes. Stir in the diced pepper and cook for a further
5 minutes.

Break the eggs into a bowl, whisk lightly and pour into the
pan. Cut the tomatoes into quarters and in half again and add to
the eggs with the luncheon meat. Season to taste and continue
cooking, stirring occasionally, until the eggs are lightly
scrambled. Serve with hot buttered toast.

Serves 4

Welsh rarebit

METRIC/IMPERIAL/AMERICAN
25 g/1 oz/2 tablespoons softened butter or margarine
1 teaspoon English or French mustard
¼ teaspoon salt
1 teaspoon grated onion
dash Worcestershire sauce
100 g/4 oz/1 cup Cheddar cheese, grated
4 slices bread
GARNISH:
watercress sprigs
slices of tomato

Cream the butter or margarine with the mustard, salt, onion,
Worcestershire sauce and cheese.

Toast the bread on one side only under the grill. Divide the
cheese mixture between the bread slices, spreading it on the
untoasted side. Cook to melt the cheese and lightly brown.
Garnish with sprigs of watercress and slices of tomatoes.

Serves 2 or 4

Egg and onion casserole

METRIC/IMPERIAL/AMERICAN
75 g/3 oz/6 tablespoons butter
225 g/8 oz/½ lb onions, sliced
175 g/6 oz/1½ cups mushrooms, washed and sliced
salt and pepper
½–1 teaspoon dried thyme
100 g/4 oz/2 cups fresh brown breadcrumbs
25 g/1 oz/¼ cup Parmesan cheese, grated
6 eggs, hard-boiled
SAUCE:
40 g/1½ oz/3 tablespoons butter
40 g/1½ oz/6 tablespoons plain flour
450 ml/¾ pint/2 cups milk
1 teaspoon made mustard
slices of tomato and parsley sprig to garnish

Melt 25 g/1 oz/2 tablespoons butter in a saucepan, add the
onion and sauté for about 10 minutes until soft. Stir in the
mushrooms and cook for 2 minutes. Add seasoning and half the
thyme. Melt remaining butter in a pan and fry breadcrumbs
until crisp and golden, allow to cool before adding the
Parmesan. Place half the crumbs in a well-greased casserole.

Melt the butter, stir in the flour and cook for 1 minute. Add
the milk. Bring to the boil, stirring. Add thyme, seasoning and
mustard. Mix with onion and mushrooms.

Slice the eggs and arrange over breadcrumbs in the casserole.
Pour the sauce over and top with remaining crumbs. Bake in the
oven (180°C, 350°F, Gas Mark 4) for 20 minutes. Garnish.

Serves 4

Cheese and pineapple flan

METRIC/IMPERIAL/AMERICAN
1 (18–20-cm/7–8-inch/7–8-inch) baked pastry flan case
100 g/4 oz/½ cup cooked bacon, diced finely
1 (200-g/7-oz/8-oz) can pineapple cubes
2 eggs, beaten
100 g/4 oz/½ cup cottage cheese
100 g/4 oz/1 cup Cheddar cheese, grated
pepper
1 teaspoon dried mustard
chopped parsley to garnish

Place the flan case on a baking sheet. Mix the bacon, drained
pineapple, eggs, cheeses, pepper and mustard together,
blending thoroughly. Pour the filling into the pastry case and
bake on centre shelf of a moderate oven (180°C, 350°F, Gas
Mark 4) for about 20–25 minutes until the filling is set. Sprinkle
with chopped parsley and serve hot or cold.

Serves 4

Cheese and mushroom noodles

METRIC/IMPERIAL/AMERICAN
40 g/1½ oz/3 tablespoons butter or margarine
1 medium onion, chopped
100 g/4 oz/1 cup mushrooms, washed and halved
1 (106-g/3¾-oz/4-oz) packet cheese slices
175 g/6 oz/6 oz ribbon noodles
salt and pepper
1 teaspoon lemon juice
chopped parsley to garnish

Melt the butter or margarine in a frying pan, add the onion and cook gently for about 10 minutes until soft. Add the mushrooms and cook for a further 2 minutes. Cut the cheese into matchstick lengths.

Meanwhile, cook the noodles in boiling salted water for about 8 minutes until just tender. Drain well and return the noodles to the pan. Stir in the cooked onion and mushroom mixture, the cheese, seasoning and lemon juice. Blend thoroughly and serve immediately, garnished with parsley.

Serves 3

Omelette layer cake

METRIC/IMPERIAL/AMERICAN
1 (198-g/7-oz/8-oz) can sweetcorn with peppers
1 (113-g/4-oz/4-oz) packet frozen peas, thawed
6 large eggs
6 tablespoons/6 tablespoons/½ cup milk
salt and pepper
3 teaspoons corn oil
2 large tomatoes, skinned and sliced
40 g/1½ oz/⅓ cup Cheddar cheese, grated

Place the sweetcorn and peas in a pan of boiling salted water. Heat gently for about 5 minutes, drain well and cool.

Break 2 eggs into each of 3 basins and add one third milk to each basin with seasoning. Heat a teaspoon oil in an omelette pan. Place a third of the vegetables into two of the basins. Pour the contents of one basin into the omelette pan, cook gently for about 5 minutes until the base is set. Place the pan under the grill to brown. Lift out on to an ovenproof plate and keep warm in the oven.

Place another teaspoon of oil in the pan, pour in the egg mixture without vegetables. Arrange tomatoes on top and cook gently to lightly brown the base, brown the top under the grill. Remove from the pan and place on the first omelette.

Make the third omelette as the first. Place on top of the other 2 omelettes. Place remaining vegetables on top, sprinkle over the cheese and heat under the grill to melt cheese.

Serves 3-4

Eggs mulligatawny

METRIC/IMPERIAL/AMERICAN
175 g/6 oz/1 cup long-grain rice
750 ml/1¼ pints/3 cups chicken stock (or water and stock
   cube)
6 large eggs, hard-boiled
SAUCE:
1 (440-g/15½-oz/16-oz) can mulligatawny soup
1 tablespoon cornflour
1 tablespoon tomato purée
2 tablespoons/2 tablespoons/3 tablespoons sweet chutney
40 g/1½ oz/4 tablespoons sultanas
watercress sprigs to garnish

Cook the rice in the boiling stock until just tender – about
12–15 minutes.

  Place the soup in a saucepan, blend the cornflour with a little
water, add to the soup with the remaining ingredients. Bring
slowly to the boil, stirring, and cook for about 5 minutes until
the cornflour thickens and clears.

  Drain the rice and arrange on a heated dish, cut the eggs into
halves lengthways and arrange on the rice. Spoon the sauce
over the eggs and garnish with watercress. Serve with
redcurrant jelly and salted peanuts, if liked.

Serves 4

Fried egg ratatouille

METRIC/IMPERIAL/AMERICAN
50 g/2 oz/¼ cup butter or margarine
2 medium onions, sliced
1 medium green pepper, deseeded and diced
1 small aubergine, sliced
350 g/12 oz/¾ lb tomatoes, peeled and chopped
1 small clove garlic, crushed (optional)
salt and pepper
4 large eggs
1 tablespoon corn oil
8 anchovy fillets to garnish

Melt the butter or margarine in a frying pan, add the onion and
cook gently until soft without browning – about 10 minutes.
Add the green pepper and aubergine and cook very slowly,
covered, for about 10 minutes without browning. Add the
tomatoes, garlic if used and seasoning.

  Fry the eggs in the oil. Arrange the vegetable mixture on a
flat heated serving dish or individual dishes. Place the eggs on
top. Garnish each egg with 2 anchovy fillets. Serve with
warmed French bread.

Serves 4

Snacks

Snack meals may be required at any time during the day, particularly during the school holidays. These recipes have been created to inspire you to prepare tasty snacks from store cupboard ingredients and convenience foods with the minimum of effort.

Pizza discs

METRIC/IMPERIAL/AMERICAN
1 medium onion, chopped
1 clove garlic (optional)
25 g/1 oz/2 tablespoons butter or margarine
1 (396-g/14-oz/14-oz) can tomatoes
1 teaspoon dried mixed herbs
salt and pepper
1 tablespoon cornflour
2 tablespoons/2 tablespoons/3 tablespoons water
10 rusks or toast rounds
100 g/4 oz/1 cup Gruyère cheese, grated
1 (56-g/2-oz/2-oz) can anchovies, drained
watercress sprigs to garnish

Place the onion, garlic and butter in a medium saucepan and cook gently for 5 minutes until soft. Drain the tomatoes and add to the pan with the dried herbs and seasoning. Stir well and simmer for 10–15 minutes until thickened. Blend the cornflour with the water, stir into the tomatoes and cook, stirring, until the cornflour has thickened and cleared.

Place the rusks on a baking sheet and divide the sauce between the biscuits spreading the mixture evenly. Top each with grated cheese. Cut the anchovy fillets in half lengthways and arrange these in a criss-cross pattern on top of each biscuit.

Place in a moderately hot oven (200°C, 400°F, Gas Mark 6) for 8–10 minutes to heat through and melt the cheese. Garnish with watercress.

Makes 10

T.V. toppers

METRIC/IMPERIAL/AMERICAN
4 rashers streaky bacon, halved
8 large flat mushrooms, washed and trimmed
4 large eggs
3 tablespoons/3 tablespoons/¼ cup milk
salt and pepper
15 g/½ oz/1 tablespoon butter or margarine
4 round crusty bread rolls, warmed
parsley sprigs to garnish

Remove the rind from the bacon rashers and roll up. Secure with a skewer and grill until slightly crisp. Put on one side and keep warm. Place the mushrooms in the pan and cook on each side for a few minutes, remove and keep warm.

Whisk together the eggs, milk and seasoning. Melt the butter or margarine in a small pan, add the eggs and heat gently, stirring until lightly scrambled.

Cut the warmed rolls in half, butter if liked and place a mushroom on each half. Divide the scrambled egg between the rolls and top each with a bacon roll. Garnish with the parsley.

Makes 8

Fried savoury scone

METRIC/IMPERIAL/AMERICAN
4 tablespoons/4 tablespoons/⅓ cup oil
50 g/2 oz/½ cup onion, chopped
1 (396-g/14-oz/14-oz) can tomatoes
½–1 teaspoon dried mixed herbs or marjoram
salt and pepper
175 g/6 oz/1½ cups self-raising flour
¼ teaspoon baking powder
25 g/1 oz/2 tablespoons margarine
5 tablespoons/5 tablespoons/6 tablespoons milk
100 g/4 oz/¼ lb pork and ham slices, in strips
2 slices processed cheese, cut into strips
3 pimento-stuffed olives, sliced, to garnish

Place 1 tablespoon of the oil in a saucepan, sauté the onion for 5 minutes. Drain the tomatoes and add to the onion with the herbs and seasoning. Cook for about 5 minutes.

Sieve the flour, baking powder and salt into a mixing bowl, rub in the margarine. Add the milk and mix until the mixture forms a fairly soft dough. Knead gently on a floured surface and roll out to a 26-cm/10-inch circle.

Heat the remaining oil in a 26-cm/10-inch frying pan. Add the dough and cook to lightly brown the base – about 3–5 minutes. Turn the pizza over and cook for the same time. Spread the tomato mixture over the dough, cover with strips of meat and cheese. Garnish and place under the grill to melt the cheese.

Serves 4

Croque monsieur

METRIC/IMPERIAL/AMERICAN
8 slices bread, 5 mm/¼ inch thick
4 cheese slices
4 tablespoons/4 tablespoons/⅓ cup corn oil
25 g/1 oz/2 tablespoons butter
GARNISH:
tomato quarters
mustard and cress

Remove the crusts from the bread keeping a good square shape. Place a cheese slice on 4 slices of bread and cover with the remaining bread slices, press down lightly.

Melt the oil and butter in a large frying pan. Fry the sandwiches in the hot fat in batches fairly quickly to brown the bread and melt the cheese. Cut each one in half. Serve immediately, garnished with the tomatoes and mustard and cress.

Serves 2–4

Scandinavian sandwiches

METRIC/IMPERIAL/AMERICAN
1 (227-g/8-oz/8-oz) packet pumpernickel bread
butter
6 lettuce leaves
6 slices liver sausage
6 slices salami
3 dill cucumbers, well drained
1 tomato, quartered
1 (225-g/8-oz/8-oz) carton potato salad
GARNISH:
mustard and cress
watercress

Separate the slices of pumpernickel and spread each slice liberally with butter. Place a lettuce leaf on each slice of bread so that it overlaps the edge a little. Divide the liver sausage and salami between the pumpernickel slices.

Cut the dill cucumbers in slices lengthways and arrange on the liver sausage with tomato quarters. Divide the potato salad and place a little in the centre of each salami slice. Garnish the sandwiches with mustard and cress and watercress.

Makes 6

Buck rarebit

METRIC/IMPERIAL/AMERICAN
4 crumpets
100 g/4 oz/1 cup Cheddar cheese, grated
oil
4 eggs
parsley sprigs to garnish

Preheat a moderate grill and toast each crumpet on both sides. Remove from the grill, divide the cheese between each crumpet then return to the grill to melt the cheese.

Meanwhile, heat the oil and fry the eggs. Place a fried egg on top of each crumpet and serve immediately. Garnish with the parsley sprigs.

Makes 4

Crispy burgers

METRIC/IMPERIAL/AMERICAN
8 slices bread
butter
4 beefburgers
horseradish sauce
stuffed olives to garnish

Cut each slice of bread with a plain round pastry cutter the same size as the beefburgers. Butter one side only. Place 4 of the buttered rounds buttered side down on a baking sheet. Place an uncooked beefburger on top, spread with a little horseradish sauce and top each with the remaining rounds of bread, buttered side uppermost.

Place on the centre shelf of a moderately hot oven (200°C, 400°F, Gas Mark 6) for 20–25 minutes. Serve hot in a paper serviette and accompany with sticks of celery and tomato wedges. Top with the stuffed olives pierced on cocktail sticks.

Makes 4

Creamed kippers

METRIC/IMPERIAL/AMERICAN
1 pair kippers
40 g/1½ oz/3 tablespoons butter or margarine
40 g/1½ oz/6 tablespoons plain flour
300 ml/½ pint/1¼ cups milk
1 egg
1 teaspoon lemon juice
4 slices toast
parsley sprigs to garnish

Poach the kippers by placing in a shallow pan of cold water. Bring to just below the boil, remove from the heat and leave for about 5 minutes. Remove the kippers and drain well. Remove the bones carefully and flake the fish.

Make the sauce by melting the butter or margarine, stir in the flour and gradually beat in the milk. Bring to the boil, stirring, and cook for about 2 minutes. Stir in the flaked kipper.

Separate the yolk from the white of the egg. Add the yolk to the fish, blending thoroughly. Whisk the egg white until stiff and fold into the mixture with the lemon juice.

Place the pieces of toast on a baking sheet, divide the mixture between them and place on the centre shelf of a moderate oven (180°C, 350°F, Gas Mark 4) for about 10–15 minutes. Serve immediately, garnished with parsley.

Serves 4

Baked bean hash

METRIC/IMPERIAL/AMERICAN
1 large onion, sliced
0.5 kg/1 lb/1 lb potatoes, peeled and diced
50 g/2 oz/¼ cup butter or margarine
1 (340-g/12-oz/12-oz) can corned beef
1 (220-g/7¾-oz/8-oz) can baked beans
1 tablespoon tomato ketchup
2 teaspoons dried mixed herbs
salt and pepper

Place the onion, potato, butter or margarine in a frying pan and sauté gently for about 20 minutes, stirring frequently.

Cut the corned beef into dice and add to the pan with the baked beans, ketchup, herbs and seasoning. Heat through gently for about 5 minutes, shaking the pan occasionally. Serve immediately.

Serves 3–4